HOW TO SUCCEED IN 12 MONTHS

D1545676

HOW TO SUCCEED IN **12** MONTHS

CREATING A LIFE YOU LOVE

SERENA STAR-LEONARD

Wrightbooks
A Wiley Brand

First published 2014 by Wrightbooks
an imprint of John Wiley & Sons Australia
42 McDougall St, Milton Qld 4064

Office also in Melbourne

Typeset in 11/13.5 pt ITC Giovanni Std

© Serena Star-Leonard 2014

The moral rights of the author have been asserted

National Library of Australia Cataloguing-in-Publication data:

Author:	Star-Leonard, Serena, author.
Title:	How to Succeed in 12 Months: creating a life you love / Serena Star-Leonard.
ISBN:	9780730308669 (pbk)
	9780730308683 (ebook)
Subjects:	Self-management (Psychology)
	Self-actualisation (Psychology)
	Change (Psychology)
	Self-help techniques
Dewey Number:	158.1

Cover design by Josh Durham, www.designbycommittee.com

Cover illustrations: Paul Dinovo

Printed in Singapore by C.O.S. Printers Pte Ltd

10 9 8 7 6 5 4 3 2 1

Disclaimer

The material in this publication is of the nature of general comment only, and neither purports nor intends to be advice. Readers should not act on the basis of any matter in this publication without considering (and if appropriate, taking) professional advice with due regard to their own particular circumstances. The author and publisher expressly disclaim all and any liability to any person, whether a purchaser of this publication or not, in respect of anything and of the consequences of anything done or omitted to be done by any such person in reliance, whether whole or partial, upon the whole or any part of the contents of this publication.

For Dorothy

For once you have tasted flight, you will forever walk with your eyes turned skywards.

Anonymous

Contents

About the author   ix
Acknowledgements   xi
Preface   xiii
Introduction   xv

 1 What is lifestyle design?   1
 2 What do you have right now?   9
 3 Goals and success   41
 4 Make the impossible, possible   51
 5 Design your life   59
 6 Take action   71
 7 Get moving   83
 8 Commitment, confidence and courage   109
 9 Time   123
10 Money   129
11 Support   149
12 Troubleshooting   163
13 Resources   181
14 Our 12-month diary   189
15 Wrapping up and moving on   203

Index   209

About the author

Serena Star-Leonard is passionate about helping people fulfil their big goals and dreams in life.

She is a Kiwi business coach, blogger and presenter, and the author of *How to Retire in 12 Months*. As well as coaching and writing, Serena runs 'Website Launchpad' courses, teaching people how to create lifestyle and income opportunities through blogging: www.in12months.com.

She is also one of the founders of Grassroots Internet Strategy, a small business resource for website owners: www.grassrootsinternetstrategy.com.au.

Serena is a keen amateur photographer, is inspired by the potential of the human spirit and is passionate about cooking and travel. She is always ready to jump in with her energy, her heart and a hot meal for those in need and is a blog ambassador for World Vision (Australia).

In hot climates, Serena loves to swim, scuba dive, snorkel and frolic in the water every chance she gets, which is pretty often as she has been travelling the world with her husband John since April 2012.

They have true location freedom and split their time between filming inspiring mini-documentaries and travel reviews for their passion project, 'Five Point Five' (www .fivepointfive.org), travelling, having adventures and writing blogs and books.

Connect with Serena:

Facebook: www.facebook.com/In12Months

Twitter: www.twitter.com/beingserenastar

LinkedIn: www.linkedin.com/in/serenastarleonard

Email: www.serena@in12months.com

Acknowledgements

This book follows our journey to create a passion project and design a life that I have daydreamed about for over a decade. We are now living that life, but appreciate that none of this would be possible without a whole community of people who have supported us at each step along the way.

My fantastic family and friends: you are so many wonderful people who are ready at every turn with laughs, inspiration, spare rooms, hot meals, crazy ideas and late-night calls. Thank you for making us feel at home all over the world.

Helen Burrows for your gorgeous partnership and keen eye in structuring and editing this book, Belle Gurd for your lovely bubbly help and expertise and everyone who shared their stories.

Thanks to my global online community. You are the innovative and courageous people who I coach, the go-getters who attend my courses, and the friendly supporters who read our newsletters and blogs and connect with me on social media. You are the core of my business and your support allows me to do what I do with my life — for this I am truly grateful.

The people we have met along the way. You were complete strangers who have opened your hearts, homes, charities, businesses and projects to us. We are now clear that food, compassion and silliness breaks all barriers of language and culture. We are constantly blown away at the warmth we enjoy everywhere, from global charities to tiny shacks in remote villages, and we are honoured that you share your personal stories with us.

The readers of *How to Retire in 12 Months*. Seeing my first book become a bestseller is something I will always treasure. To all the fantastic people who bought, borrowed or gifted the book, thank you for your support, for taking the time to write reviews, and for the personal stories you have shared with me.

Last, but in no way least, my soul mate, husband, business partner, documentary film director and lifelong travel buddy John Leonard. Thanks for making every day an adventure.

Preface

In 2011, my book *How to Retire in 12 Months* came out in Australasia. It is a motivational business book that focuses on the art of blogging as a means of creating an income. Blogging is not for everyone, however, and I have many clients who are looking for alternative options for retiring, creating their dream lifestyle, or achieving important goals they are afraid to embark upon.

This sequel, *How to Succeed in 12 Months: Creating a Life You Love*, is designed to enable you to achieve all your big dreams. Whether you want to travel the world, start a business, make a difference or change the way you live your life, this book is for you.

The strategy behind my success (and yours) is based around acting on the big goals and dreams that many people ignore. It is taking action that will enable you to achieve the things that are important to you.

The book is designed to share what I learned through hard work, luck and dogged persistence. I have a passion for making complex, seemingly impossible ideas and dreams achievable, and I am thrilled to share what I have learned with you.

Serena Star-Leonard

Introduction

Why this book?

I dream of a world where this book is not necessary. Where people know from an early age that anything is possible if they only try and don't give up. We are born with this notion, yet somewhere along the way we stop believing in ourselves and, as a result, we stop living like we can achieve anything.

Instead, we look up to people who are successful and who have confidence in their abilities. We aspire to be like these people, but at the same time we hold ourselves back by not believing that maybe we could achieve our own big goals too.

The main reasons why many of us don't achieve our lifelong dreams are because we either don't start, or we give up too quickly. It is no surprise, therefore, that the most successful people are often the most persistent.

This book is for anyone looking for a fulfilling life. It is for people who want to create the things most people only dream of. It is for people who want to achieve exciting goals, or at least be satisfied that they gave those goals their best shot. It is not about waiting for the right time or for any ducks or planets to align before becoming someone who makes those dreams a reality; it is about being that person right now. I hope that by sharing the things I learned along the way and the things I wish I had known when I wanted to start realising my own dreams, I can save you some of the effort and angst I experienced in my own journey.

If you are ready, we are going to take a journey along the road to creating and living your dream life. To assist you, I set out all the steps you will need to take and introduce practical resources along the way.

Note: Throughout the book I have included tasks that you can do to work directly on your life-changing project. Find an exercise book or open a folder on your computer to keep your project 'work' in one place. I have set up a page with additional resources to complement the exercises in this book. Visit www.in12months.com/readers and use the password 'success'.

Why 12 months?

Considering the name and theme of both of my books, you can correctly assume that I am a big fan of 12-month projects. Twelve months is long enough to completely alter your life, but not so long that you grow old in the process (physically anyway!). You can achieve great things in 12 months, but it will go by really quickly when you are in the heart of the action.

Of course, you could fulfil some of your dreams much sooner than 12 months, while others may take years to come to fruition. There is no right amount of time. What you can be certain of is that if you give yourself 12 months to make a big, exciting dream project a reality, it may just happen and you will be living the life you always dreamed of — or at least you will be much closer to it than if you had done nothing at all.

In 2009 I began my first 12-month, life-changing project: to create an income I could earn working one day a week from anywhere in the world. Achieving this goal allowed me to create exciting, new 12-month goals.

Throughout the book I am going to share my progress on a 12-month adventure my husband and I conceived that resulted in us living a creative travel lifestyle we have designed for ourselves.

It is more than just an adventure; we now — for the first time in our lives — choose every part of our lives. Even though we are both very liberal in our philosophies and open-minded about how we live, we have until recently spent our lives working hard in normal jobs/small businesses, renting apartments and generally being stuck in a (comfortable) rut. We were conforming non-conformists, where our lifestyle did not fit our ideals, but we didn't notice how much it didn't fit because we were so busy conforming!

This latest 12-month project was based on our thirst to be inspired, see the world and make a difference. We created a project and website called 'Five Point Five', which seeks out inspirational people and their wonderful community projects throughout the world.

We share their stories using five-minute documentaries so that our audience can have a quick shot of inspiration, to see people from all walks of life making a difference.

We wanted to create and use mobile incomes to cover our costs, and to review hotels and tours to cut our expenses and enable us to stay in amazing places and enjoy exciting adventures year round. Before we started, we had no experience with any of what we were about to do, but 12 months in, we have achieved our goal and have since continued living the dream.

It took a few months of this new life and lifestyle before we started to notice how creative, calm and happy we had become. Not just because we are travelling through wonderful places, but because we have taken control of how we live our lives. The change has given us far more freedom than we had ever imagined possible.

Whether you are 25, 49, 63 or 90, you have a unique opportunity to take control of the direction of your life over the next 12 months. If you really go for it, what happens may completely change your experience of yourself, your life and the world around you.

Outrageous expectations

We live in a society where our expectations about life are heavily influenced by television, movies, magazines, newspapers and the internet. There is a growing youth culture looking for something for nothing and the easy way to get it—and it is not only the youth who are affected by it. Some of the most popular shows on television showcase super-rich kids, or glorify the lifestyle of super-rich actors, sports stars and entrepreneurs. You can see fancy cars, perfect bodies and young divas whose only claim to fame is the bank balance of their parents.

I see pre-teens watch talent shows and fixate on the possibility of instant global fame and fortune. In past generations one might have hoped to win the lottery, but there is a new message for today's youth: you can be an overnight success, recognised as the amazing, talented and immensely special person that you really are. Add to that the messages of the majority of commercial music, music videos and Hollywood films and I think the reality of hard slog in entry-level jobs may make adulthood look like a major comedown.

As adults, we tend to follow big success stories. Many years ago it was Silicon Valley, dotcoms and the promise of multilevel marketing. More recently it is the makers of the big apps, search engines and social media websites.

These stories make front-page news because many people are looking for overnight success — the easy win and the big money. Sadly though, the majority of people will not reach these dreams.

The thing with outrageous expectations is that if you are not doing everything you can to live up to them, they are going to leave you unfulfilled, unhappy and looking for an escape. Unfortunately many people do escape, but not in a healthy way, instead using drugs, alcohol, television or excess food, becoming cynical or resigned, or all of the above.

There is nothing wrong with having huge goals if you are willing to do what it takes to make them a reality. If your expectations come with any false sense of entitlement or hope that they will fall in your lap, you are going to be disappointed.

Spend a few years disappointed with your life and, like most people, you will tend to go the same way, sinking into a quiet malaise of resignation. Even some of the most confident, happy and positive people have an underlying resignation about what is possible in their own lives.

Make friends with failure

It may seem weird to talk about failure before we get to the juicy stuff. However, I think our attitudes to failure are so important that we just have to talk about it now.

The fact is, you will fail sometimes. It happens. Then you will succeed sometimes, then you will fail sometimes, then you will succeed. The important thing is that failure is integral to success, but for the most part, in modern society we are trained to avoid it. As such, many of us spend our lives actively avoiding our big dreams in case we work towards them and fail. This leaves us in a bind because life when you are ignoring your dreams is very unsatisfying.

After a few years of living this way, most of us become resigned to accepting what we have and making the best of life with our self-imposed limitations. There is nothing wrong with that, of course, but it means that our dream lives never become a reality and our dreams are seldom fulfilled.

In order to be someone who feels the freedom to follow your dreams, you need to retrain your attitude to failure. To do so, you will need to embrace failure as just part of the journey. Although it can be a very painful part of the journey sometimes, it has its benefits, which include:

- learning what not to do and what doesn't work
- learning important lessons that you wouldn't otherwise learn
- getting a chance to start again, or in a different way
- seeing how determined, strong and persistent you really are.

I am sure you can think of plenty more benefits of failure. If you scratch the surface of every success story you will find many failures. Some people will fail at some things while succeeding at others. For example, some people fail at sustaining intimate relationships, while having great success in business.

If you are ready to reconsider your attitude to failure and accept it as part of the journey, then we are at the right place to proceed in designing your life and making your dreams come true.

Success

The reason we need to be willing to risk failure is that there is the possibility of great success! The greater your goal, the greater the risk, and the greater the reward if you make it work.

What makes success so sweet is that it is not guaranteed, so the more times you fail, the sweeter it is when you are successful. Success looks completely different for different people, and often it doesn't end up looking how you imagined it.

The experience of succeeding in your goals and projects helps you grow in confidence and courage, and it can open up a whole new world of amazing goals and projects to take on!

When I started a blog I had no idea what to expect, but when people started to follow it and read it, the opportunity of a book deal was created. Writing and launching the book created the opportunity of running a course, which in turn created the opportunity of taking my business around the world. By travelling the world, the opportunity of reviewing exciting tours, cruises and lush hotels was created, along with the opportunity of visiting amazing community projects and producing mini-documentaries. None of this would have been possible if I had not taken action and started the first blog!

The success my husband and I now enjoy daily is that we live with a feeling of freedom and adventure. In my experience, however, each success is a fleeting cause for celebration; the real reward for us has been the lifestyle we now live and the exciting new opportunities that continue to open up along the way.

For some, success may look like creating their own space of peace where they can relax and meditate. For others, success may look like an intense, high-powered job or business where they get to make a lot of money or create and impact big things in the world.

Because success is completely subjective, we often have a terrible habit of looking at other 'successful' people and comparing ourselves to them. For many people, particularly in Western societies, there will always be more we can do and have. The opportunity you have is to set your own dreams and goals, make them happen, and appreciate them when you reach them. Do this and you will find as much happiness and fulfillment as all the successful people you could ever compare yourself to.

Redefining success

So this is the bit where I redefine success. I feel it is important to redefine *success* and *succeeding* because for most people the idea of success is tied to wealth and money. The problem with this idea of success is that the current financial systems and global resources are not designed to allow the majority of people to be wealthy, so most people in the world will not experience success the way it is sold through the mass media.

The systems do not work to enrich or empower the general population and this is where I take exception to the common notion of success.

When I started out in business, I had plenty of passion and big ideas. But with no experience, no mentors and a healthy dose of limiting beliefs, it was likely I was going to have a roller-coaster of an experience. I did. At one point I ran a festival with a group of volunteers and I was hoping for 1500 people to attend. When more than 8000 people came, it took me a couple of days to allow myself to feel that it was a success, because I was focused on how it could have been better. But once I reviewed it objectively, I saw that it probably could not have gone much better and I realised I had run a successful festival!

The following year we ran the festival again with big plans to expand, but we didn't have some of the important factors we had the year before and only 4000 people came. If the first year had not been so huge the second year would have been a fantastic result. But because fewer people attended than the previous year, I felt that I had failed and carried forward a huge sense of disappointment.

After this I set up a few charity projects, businesses and many other passion projects. Some of these I worked on very hard and they failed. Some I lost my passion for. Some were successful and have become the core of my lifestyle today. Some I didn't really have the capacity for, but I was so excited about all the things I could be part of that I would start far more projects than I had the time, energy or resources for.

In this period of wild energy, personal growth and sometimes fruitless hard work I met hundreds of people who came in and out of my projects, businesses and social life. I am sure that many of them have very different perceptions of me and my levels of success and failure.

I heard from one friend that I had tried too many things and she no longer thought I would ever *succeed*. The word cut through me like a knife — the sting of a world that is conditioned to be afraid to fail.

My dislike for the common notion of success is that it is all about the destination rather than the journey, and success as a destination is only short-lived. In the traditional sense, success is usually something you have reached — or not — and in the traditional sense, it can be outgrown, outlived, spent or taken away.

I believe that the journey, the adventure, striding boldly forth into the unknown, is where you develop lifelong skills for creating continued success. The journey is where the success lies because you are making every moment count.

True success is a measure of whether you are making the most of the life you have right now, today, in this moment. Today is where a life of happiness, adventure and fulfilment is possible. I love Anthony Robbins's quote, 'Success is doing what you want to do, when you want, where you want, with whom you want, as much as you want'.

Living with this level of freedom is a beautiful thing.

Chapter 1

What is lifestyle design?

The concept of lifestyle design has been around for decades, but it became a global phenomenon following the success of Timothy Ferriss's book *The 4-Hour Workweek*.

Lifestyle design is the art of creating a fulfilling lifestyle *now*, rather than waiting for retirement or some unexpected windfall.

Lifestyle design does not look the same for any two people, or even for any two different stages of life. Some people have a passion they can fulfil for their entire lives. Other people discover new passions over and over throughout their lives.

Right now my lifestyle is designed to enable me to travel long-term and have time to immerse myself in whatever project I am currently inspired by. In a couple of years my dream lifestyle will most likely be different because I will want to spend my time with the children I would like to have.

The starting block is the life you are living right now. This is the foundation upon which you can design the life you choose to live. Like me, not many people will start designing their dream lives on a blank canvas. The majority of us have pre-existing responsibilities (such as children, family, debts or a business) and things that we like, dislike or are profoundly passionate about.

How we design our lives is based on our passions and responsibilities. The life you design could involve:

⇨ quitting a job to start a business

⇨ creating an alternative income, enabling you to spend more time with your children/family

⇨ working from home or in other countries

⇨ working less

⇨ travelling more

⇨ committing your time/life to making a difference

⇨ scoring your dream job or changing career

⇨ going full-time with your hobby

⇨ starting community projects

⇨ living sustainably and/or off the grid.

The options are endless.

A life of freedom

My experience of living a life I've designed is a recent achievement.

I am writing this from a gorgeous apartment in Bolivia, with views across the city to snow-capped mountains. My husband and I have been travelling for more than one and a half years. About six months into our trip I realised that I was used to this lifestyle. I now accept that visiting amazing places and meeting inspiring people is my everyday life. It feels normal to wake up each day and decide what we are going to do, be it going to the beach, visiting a ruin, learning something new, working on one of the many projects we are involved in, or writing a blog or book!

We have designed our life to fulfil our passions and goals. We are not afraid to have big goals. We accept that we may succeed or fail, but we give each of them our best shot.

Although this life is normal now, I still pinch myself occasionally because this lifestyle seemed impossible for most of my life. I say *seemed impossible* because once we took a series of actions towards achieving our goal, it all became very possible.

At many times in the past I had been resigned to how things were, even when a lot of things sucked, such as:

- long commutes to work sitting in traffic
- working long hours for my employer
- being scared to leave my job
- when I did leave my job, spending a few years working long hours, seven days a week on my businesses
- having huge debts
- earning very little and having no financial security
- being single and lonely
- failing at many things I tried
- not looking after my health.

You can see why getting used to my new life of love, travel and adventure is pretty thrilling!

It wasn't easy getting here, however. I have worked very hard and invested a lot of time and energy on projects, goals, businesses and charities—learning and trying, over and over again. I have worn myself out at times trying to figure out how to free myself from the shackles of the life I had, in order to live a life I love.

The problem was that I didn't know it was *freedom* that I was looking for. In hindsight, it is obvious and I can see that it didn't need to be so hard to figure out.

Freedom mindset

It is very easy to understand and adopt a sense of freedom when you have been travelling for as long as we have. But the mindset is possible whether you travel or not. It is something you can cultivate even if you are bedridden, or have never left the country you were born in. The experience of freedom comes when you realise that you call the shots in your life. There are many situations where you may not feel this to be true, where you may feel trapped or constrained. But you do have choices, whether you can see them or not. They may not necessarily be choices that you like all the time, but they are choices nonetheless.

Sadly, we are not taught how to develop our freedom mindset at the schools that most of us attend. Although many people aspire to live with this mindset, most people believe in some way that it is something possible for other people, but not possible for them. This is not true. It is possible to create freedom in your life by simply realising that you are free. You *are* able to do fantastic and exciting things with your life.

The problem for many people is that with freedom comes great responsibility. To be free you must accept that you are responsible for your life—that you are creating it, whether you realise it or not. Many people blame their parents, boss, partner, kids, health, the government or anything or anyone else for how unhappy and unsatisfied they are. The fundamental flaw in blaming others is that you are giving others an invisible hold over you. You are giving away your power to be free.

Don't get me wrong, things will happen to you that are outside your control; many tragic and wonderful things will probably happen in your lifetime that you have no control over.

But you do control your reactions to these things. You do control how you view and act in the world around you, and the situations you are faced with. This is how you create your world; this is where your true freedom lies.

Creating a freedom mindset is something that you can do, and for most people it means a dramatic change in how you see the world. The self-help industry is enormous because there are millions of people out there looking for more out of life and wanting to learn the elusive secret of how to be truly happy, fulfilled and free.

In my experience there is a shortcut. The quickest way to create a life of freedom and fulfilment is to be bold and work hard to do what it takes to fulfil your dreams now, even if they seem impossible.

Throughout this book I am going to share with you stories of real, everyday people who had a moment of clarity and decided to take life into their own hands. They were people just like you, with lives just like yours. Each one of them reached a point where they saw they had to take action to make their dreams a reality, even if their dreams seemed impossible and they had no idea how to make them happen.

I hope you take inspiration from their stories when you embark on your own life-changing adventure. I begin with Lee's story.

Case study: a late start in the music industry

Lee Safar has always had a passion for music. She played instruments from a young age and found she had a natural talent. She was brought up to be a good girl who followed the rules, so when she left school she was devastated to learn that her family's cultural beliefs did not align with her dreams to be a musician. At 17 Lee gave up music and followed a mainstream path of university and then senior jobs in the corporate world.

After repressing her dream for more than a decade, Lee one day realised she had to make a change because her life *had* to be about music. Music was her passion and she could no longer hide, blaming her parents for not allowing her to pursue her dream. She realised she was responsible for her life and how it would turn out.

Lee got into action and booked a singing coach. She learned to play the guitar and the piano and took the opportunity to do open-microphone nights and gigs around Sydney. She started writing songs and eventually quit her corporate job to work part-time as a barista so that she would have more time for her music.

Lee takes every opportunity to speak to people in the industry and learn as much as she can. She has recorded two EPs and a full album. She feels alive because she owns every decision she makes and, for the first time, believes in the possibility of her lifelong dream being a reality.

Now Lee splits her time between Sydney and Los Angeles as she develops her music career and empowers other musicians with the creation of a regular web-based music-industry show on her website, **www.leesafar.com**

What you need to succeed

There are certain types of people who are more likely to make their dreams come true. These people are not born this way and there is no genetic relationship between them. It is a mindset shift that occurs at some point in some people's lives. I like to call it a Good Life Crisis.

A Good Life Crisis is when you look at your life and think, 'If I continue on the path I am on, my life is going to be more of what it is already'. If your path looks dreary, hard or boring, with no exciting goals ahead, then you may experience an inner fire to alter your life dramatically — a motivator for change that is almost too insistent to ignore.

Emotionally there are three stages that lead to a Good Life Crisis:

✎ *Feeling stuck, bored, hopeless or depressed.* This stage is tough because it feels like you are trapped, you have no control over your life and everyone else is having a better time than you. You will notice everything that sucks about your life and you may fixate on how awful certain people — such as a boss, a friend, a family member or a past or current partner — are.

✎ *Feeling that there is more out there but being unsure how to access it.* This is the stage where you notice the success of inspiring people in the news, friends of friends, and so on. Your ears prick up because you are excited about the possibility of something happening in your own life, but you lack the self-confidence to make it happen. You are pretty sure that they have something you don't and that although you would love change, you don't believe you can make it happen. You have some dreams, but they seem impossible.

➭ *Feeling motivated to take action.* When you reach this stage you will find yourself looking for opportunities. You may know what it is you want to do or change (or at least have a general idea). You find yourself doing things you wouldn't normally do, or taking on new challenges, reading related books, doing courses and being drawn to new people or communities. This is the stage where you start to create a new way of life, and however scared or uncertain you may be, your determination to create change propels you into a new way of life.

You may experience any one or all three stages when approaching a Good Life Crisis. Each person is different. But what is the same is the point when you start to take action. If you are reading this book, it is likely that you are looking for more out of life and are willing to do something exciting and extraordinary with your life. It's up to you whether you start to take action on making your dreams a reality today or in 5, 10 or 30 years' time.

In my experience, there are some important elements that contribute to the likelihood of success. They are:

➭ a supportive, like-minded community

➭ a public declaration of your goal/s

➭ deadlines

➭ coaches and mentors

➭ your commitment to do what it takes.

This book and its accompanying resources address the first four items in this list. The fifth is up to you.

Chapter 2

What do you have right now?

In order to track your progress over time, it's important to establish where you are right now. To do this we're going to create a benchmark for your life as it stands at this moment. We often drift through life without taking stock of what we've achieved, what we can be grateful for and what we tolerate that could be improved.

For this reason I've created a Lifestyle Checklist.

Lifestyle Checklist

Does your life tick all the boxes?

When was the last time you reviewed exactly where you are in life? We live in a world of wanting more, more and more. This is not inherently wrong, but it prevents us from appreciating what we already have.

The Lifestyle Checklist is designed to help you see what is working and what is not working in your life right now.

While going through the Lifestyle Checklist, start to think about the areas of your life that are going really well and the areas where you would like to see an improvement. It will show you the big picture of your life, which is something most of us rarely or never see.

Too often we focus on one or two areas of our lives and ignore the rest. Having this kind of microfocus can mean that we feel everything is wrong when in fact only one or two areas are not working. Conversely, we can become absorbed in the success of one area of our life when everything else is crashing down around us.

Understanding where you are right now will give you something to measure your progress against when you start on the road to making your big dreams a reality. Keep your score and redo the exercise periodically over the next 12 months. It will be interesting to see how your scores change.

In each part of the Lifestyle Checklist there is a series of questions that will help you determine your score. Get a pen for recording your scores. For each:

➪ 'No', give yourself a 0

➪ 'Somewhat', give yourself a 1

➪ 'Yes', give yourself a 2.

Relationships checklist

Relationships	No (0 points)	Somewhat (1 point)	Yes (2 points)
Family			
Do you have a family that contributes to your happiness and cares for your wellbeing?			
Friends			
Do you have close friends who understand and support you?			
Mentors			
Do you have inspiring mentors who are committed to helping you strive for your goals?			
Partnerships and love			
Do you have a partner who loves and supports you through the joys and challenges of life?			
Contribution			
Are there people who rely on you for emotional support and guidance?			
Leadership			
Are there people who look up to you as a leader or role model?			
Community			
Are you part of any communities (e.g. work, religious, online, charity) that you contribute to and that appreciate you for who you are?			

Total score (add up all your points): _____

What does your points total say about your relationships?

Now take your points total from the relationships checklist and read the section that corresponds to your score.

0–5 points

It may be time for a reality check. Whether you like it or not, your relationship with yourself and with others provides you with the foundation for an amazing life. However, it would seem that you think you are misunderstood, unsupported or unimportant to the people around you.

If this is the case, here are some ideas for altering your relationships for the better, including the relationship with yourself.

1   Look at who you can make more of a contribution to and how. Make it your business to make that contribution.

2   Call or visit someone every day who you love and remind them why you love them.

3   Volunteer regularly to assist a person or group that needs your help. For example:

  —   mow the grass for an elderly neighbour

  —   volunteer with a charity that does work you are interested in

  —   babysit for a busy mum.

4   Consider why your relationships are the way they are. Look at how you may have been responsible for them souring. Contact those people and apologise.

5   Make an effort in all the ways you usually avoid making an effort. If you can confess to being slack and make a new promise to the person involved, do so.

6   Try for a month to be a 'yes' person. That is, say 'yes' to things you would normally say 'no' to.

7   Book in for courses and read books on personal development or meditation. Take on different perspectives and the whole world will open up to you.

The more you contribute to your community and the people around you, the more you will get back. Get out there and make each day a day where you make a difference to someone. You may just find that this positively impacts many other areas of your life as well.

6–10 points

You have some great relationships and there are probably some areas where you could improve. The more people you contribute to, and the more people you let contribute to you, the better your support network and quality of life.

Take some time to reflect on your relationships. Here are some questions that will get you thinking.

1   When was the last time you told important people in your life why you love them?

2   Are there any people you take for granted?

3   What is it about your great relationships that makes them so great? Could you extend those qualities to some of your other relationships?

4   Look at any imbalances:

   – Do you rely on many people?

   – Do many people rely on you?

   – Are you primarily reliant, or primarily relied upon?

(continued)

What does your points total say about your relationships? *(cont'd)*

5   Are there some niggly things that keep coming up which you could view differently and resolve about the relationships you have with others or with yourself?

6   Is there something you have been meaning to do that you never got around to doing?

7   Do you surround yourself with people who will help you move in the direction you want to go? Sometimes you need to let new people into your life to get the support and understanding you need.

11–14 points

Congratulations! You have lots of great relationships and a solid support network. Your ability to create and maintain strong relationships in all facets of life will greatly contribute to your overall quality of life.

You contribute to people on a regular basis and allow others to contribute to you too. You are probably a good role model and someone who helps, inspires and/or entertains the people around you.

Understand that not everyone has this skill, and with it you increase your chances of success in everything you do. So make the most of it!

Finances checklist

Finances	No (0 points)	Somewhat (1 point)	Yes (2 points)
Income			
Do you have a regular income that covers your living expenses?			
Savings			
Do you have enough savings to survive an unexpected cost or life change?			
Property			
Do you have an investment in property?			
Other investments			
Do you have other types of investments that contribute to your financial security?			
Budget			
Do you have a budget or a clear idea of your general spending and financial goals?			
Confidence			
Are you clearly moving forward towards your financial goals?			

Total score (add up all your points): _____

What does your points total say about your finances?

Now take your points total from the finances checklist and read the section that corresponds to your score.

0–4 points

You may have a lot of great things going for you in life, but your finances leave something to be desired.

There are many reasons why you could be in this category. You may be just getting started and have not had any opportunities yet to set yourself up. You may have been unlucky in business, life or with your investments. You may be financially irresponsible or you may have invested everything you own into something that is yet to come to fruition.

It is important to understand why your financial position is limited. If you are someone who takes big risks, you may find yourself in this situation at different stages in your life, and that is part of the risk you are taking to get ahead. You can't really judge the bad times as the be-all and end-all. Instead, view this as a glitch in your life that you can resurrect. (If, however, this becomes a common pattern in your life, the tips below may help too.)

Conversely, if you are someone who is always struggling and you don't feel you have the tools or motivation to change how you live your life, then it is time to make a change!

1   Educate yourself financially. Read books; do courses; talk to someone who can help you learn the basics of being financially healthy.

2   Find yourself a financial coach or mentor, someone you can work with and report to on your progress.

3   Analyse your patterns. It helps to get an outside perspective, someone who can help you identify the impact that your lack of financial smarts is having on

your life. You may have emotional issues about money that are dictating your actions or inaction. This being the case, you may find counselling or personal development can help you create more rewarding patterns.

4   Record all of the spending and earning in your life — it doesn't matter if it is in a spreadsheet, an app or a notebook. Writing down your expenditure will help you become more aware of where your money comes from and goes to, and potentially see where you can make changes.

5   Set yourself a life-changing financial challenge and immerse yourself in that specific area. The more familiar you are with how things work, the less scary and impossible they will seem.

5–9 points

You are on your way! You have some financial smarts and are doing what you can to grow your wealth and security. You are strong in some areas, and can see other ways of setting yourself up to create and make the most of the opportunities that come your way.

You probably have a plan for where you would like to grow, and are working on achieving that.

By global standards you are wealthy and in a fantastic position, so make the most of your hard work and good fortune and continue to do what you are doing.

If you are dealing with debt, acknowledge how far you have come and the lessons you have learned along the way.

10–12 points

Congratulations! You are in a financial position that most people only dream of. Whether you have worked hard to get this far, or are the recipient of good fortune, be grateful that

(continued)

What does your points total say about your finances? *(cont'd)*

you can now live without the major worry that many people carry in their lives.

It is important though to notice how your other section results compare. If you are in the top bracket of many of them, you are on your way to the Holy Grail of an amazing life. However, if you are lacking in many areas, especially relationships, health or quality of life, take a step back and look at how you can have it all.

Business/career checklist

Business/career	No (0 points)	Somewhat (1 point)	Yes (2 points)
Options for growth			
Do you have a job or business that gives you clear options for growth or forward momentum?			
Satisfaction			
Do you enjoy the work you do?			
Appreciation			
Are you appreciated by your colleagues, employer, clients or customers?			
Fall back			
Do you have transferable skills should your current business or job not work out?			
Learning			
Are you challenged through learning new skills, and gaining knowledge and confidence?			
Total score (add up all your points): _____			

What does your points total say about your business/career?

Now take the points total from the business/career checklist and read the section that corresponds to your score.

0–3 points

If you are just starting out, restarting, unemployed or on a path that doesn't suit you, you will not have expected to score highly in this section. But, if you are genuinely stuck in a career rut there is good news: you can make a change! Your business or career is probably what you spend most of your waking time working on, so life is much sweeter when you love what you do. If you have been doing the same thing for a long time, it can be terrifying to even think about change. But consider this: this time next year you could be involved in something you are truly passionate about and have 12 months' experience under your belt. Or, you could be doing what you are doing right now. What would you prefer?

Here are some tips for making the most of it.

1   Get clear about what you did to get to this point in your life—the good and the bad. Have you been afraid of change? Have you let other people call the shots? Have you been lazy?

2   Get clear on what you really want to be doing. Many times we continue along our existing path because we haven't thought of what we really want to do. Write a comprehensive list of:

   –   the skills you have

   –   what you know or have experience in

   –   what you are passionate about

   –   what you would love to be doing with your life if you could.

(continued)

What does your points total say about your business/career? *(cont'd)*

3   Talk to people about what you want, especially if you know people who are doing what you want to do. There are possible opportunities and inspiration in every conversation.

4   Consider five key actions you could take to get closer to the business or career you want.

5   Take those actions.

6   Repeat steps 4 and 5 until you get the results you are looking for.

4–7 points

You are on your way! There are probably areas in which you are looking to change or expand, and things may not be perfect, but you have some confidence in your abilities and room to move and grow. You have a solid foundation within yourself and what you are doing to have the potential for great fulfilment, and you should have the confidence to back yourself when choosing the direction of your future paths.

8–10 points

You are doing all the right things. You are probably on a path you have chosen. You have worked hard and are grateful for the opportunities you have created for yourself. If you have scored high in other areas of your life, you are living the dream! To feel satisfaction and fulfilment in this area as well as in your relationships means you have balance and the best of both worlds. If there is no balance and you are working yourself to the bone, look at how you can bring the same focus and priority to other areas of your life as well.

Quality-of-life checklist

Quality of life	No (0 points)	Somewhat (1 point)	Yes (2 points)
Security			
Do you live in a safe environment?			
Time			
Do you feel you have a good balance between work time and personal time?			
Stress			
Are you able to manage your work and responsibilities calmly and confidently most of the time?			
Time with family, friends and heroes			
Do you get to spend as much time as you would like with the people you love and/or admire?			
Comfort			
Do you have a comfortable home and/or living space?			
Total score (add up all your points): _____			

What does your points total say about your quality of life?

Now take your points total from the quality-of-life checklist and read the section that corresponds to your score.

0–3 points

You are most likely experiencing several areas of recurrent discomfort and stress in your day-to-day life. Even the most tolerant and relaxed people can crack when there is discomfort in too many areas, and you have a high level of dissatisfaction about the important aspects of your life. Your quality of life is the foundation upon which you work, dream, create and achieve. If your foundation is rocky it is likely to affect your ability to make magic.

Don't despair, however. All of these things can be temporary and are often the things that give you mental toughness and new levels of tolerance.

If you are very young, or are actively working on changes in your life, these things are just part of the journey. However, if you find yourself in a rut with no light at the end of the tunnel, here are some tips for getting started on your new life.

1   Write a list of what you have versus what you want. You will probably see some things that you could change straight away or in the not-too-distant future. If you can't see how to make changes, work through this list with someone who will see things from a different perspective and could point you in a new direction.

2   Look at what has got you to this point. Many people will struggle with this, but if you are going to take responsibility for your life, now is a good time to start. You have been thinking and behaving a certain way up to this moment and the result is your existing life. If you allow yourself to think and behave in a different way, you will get a different experience of life.

There is a wealth of books, courses and philosophies that will help you explore this concept.

3   Look at what is important to you in life as a series of projects. Then start, one project at a time, to improve the quality of your life overall. For example, you may decide that for you, your quality of life depends on 'loving my living space', 'spending time with loved ones', 'making dreams happen', 'having amazing relationships', 'painting regularly', 'business or career advancement', 'becoming fit and healthy' and 'daily belly laughing'. You may not be able to impact everything at once, but you can take small actions on one, two or three areas each day. Small actions in the areas that are important to you can make a huge difference to your experience of life.

4–7 points

You have a good quality of life and you can see some things that would make it even better. As you go through life, these things may ebb and flow, but if you can maintain some balance, you will give yourself a good foundation for working on designing your life and increasing your score in this area.

8–10 points

You have a great quality of life. Having these fundamental things covered much of the time will give you a great grounding for taking action on what is important to you in life.

If you fall into this category but find you still stress about everyday things, you need to find a way to let go. You have a better quality of life than most people in the world, so focus on what you have and what is going right, rather than on what you don't have or can't control.

The only downfall for some people in this category is that if you are too comfortable, you may be less willing to take risks! If you have an unfulfilled desire, don't be afraid to chase it.

Personal satisfaction checklist

Personal satisfaction	No (0 points)	Somewhat (1 point)	Yes (2 points)
Fulfilment			
Do you feel happy and fulfilled?			
Commitment			
To the best of your ability, are you doing what you are committed to?			
Passion			
Do you pursue many of your passions in life?			
Learning and challenges			
Do you challenge yourself to learn new things (big or small) on a regular basis?			
Priorities			
Does it feel like you have what is important to you right now?			
Life path			
Do you feel you are on a life journey that is fulfilling your potential?			
Total score (add up all your points): _____			

What does your points total say about your personal satisfaction?

Now take your points total from the personal satisfaction checklist and read the section that corresponds to your score.

0–4 points

You are probably feeling stuck in a rut and may be resigned to having an unfulfilling life. Even though you know other people who do amazing things, you don't feel you can make this happen in your own life. Being low in satisfaction usually comes when you have a settled style of life. You follow a routine for work (or no work), for your social life and for life in general. People in this category tend to watch a lot of television and be self-deprecating, and are less likely to look after their general health and wellbeing.

You are here because you have not taken many chances, so you do not see the vast wealth of opportunities available to you. This may be a result of social conditioning or because you have deep-seated insecurities about your ability and potential. Either way, the good news is that all this can change. You will benefit most from finding a source of motivation and support that will hold your hand until you have the confidence to dream and then make those dreams a reality.

(continued)

What does your points total say about your personal satisfaction? *(cont'd)*

Here are some tips.

1 *Immerse yourself in a new philosophy.* To create a positive and motivated mindset it helps to throw yourself into a new environment that will help you discover and live with a healthy and more adventurous outlook on life. Depending on your personality, you may find this in books; personal development courses; peer or business groups; or with counselling, coaching or mentoring...or all of the above.

2 *Shake things up.* Challenge yourself to do something different every day. Try new foods. Get up early and walk down to a park or the beach and enjoy a new part of the day. Call people you haven't spoken to for a while and get reacquainted. Say 'yes' to things you would normally say 'no' to. Buy some clothes you feel fabulous in. Get physical in new ways. Basically do whatever you can to quit your routine and embrace spontaneity and a new lease on life. This is a great transition to being someone who follows their dreams.

3 *Alter your self-talk.* Start to notice every time the conversation going on in your head is limiting, negative and/or judgemental and then deliberately replace it with a positive or empowering thought or affirmation. To open up the doors of possibility you need to retrain your brain to habitually see what is good and what is possible, while quieting the automated negative and disempowering thoughts.

5–8 points

Life is pretty good and you don't have much to complain about. Only a couple of areas of your life are somewhat unfulfilling. Although you daydream about what is possible, you are probably not taking serious steps towards making those big dreams a reality. This can be a danger zone for most people as a comfortable life may stop you from following your big dreams. You may be reaching goals and feeling settled, so why rock the boat?

This is where a lot of people stop and relax, because although their lives are constrained in some ways—maybe by a dissatisfying job—they still have a lot of things going for them that offset the boredom, pain or frustration. You may look at the reasons why you should stick with what you have rather than taking your life to the next level, because it is easier to be with the devil you know.

However, in this situation you are uniquely positioned to create an amazing, thrilling life, because you are already so close. You have a foundation on which to build. Take it to the next level and see your life spill over in personal achievement and satisfaction.

9–12 points

You are making the most out of life! You are willing to challenge yourself and work towards the exciting goals you set for yourself. You understand that life is a journey and you are making the journey count. Regardless of your financial situation, you are rich with the essence of life and can enjoy riches that many people will never experience—in the form of true fulfilment and an understanding that you are in the driver's seat of your life.

Health checklist

Health	No (0 points)	Somewhat (1 point)	Yes (2 points)
Health and wellbeing			
Would you consider yourself to be a healthy person?			
Food and consumption			
Is your body powered by a variety of healthy food and drink?			
Healthy options			
Do you avoid unhealthy food, alcohol, chemicals and cigarettes wherever possible?			
Sleep			
Do you get enough sleep to feel rested each day?			
Energy			
Are you able to sustain your energy throughout the day without stimulants such as caffeine and sugar?			
Fitness			
Do you exercise for at least 30 minutes, four or more days a week?			
Mindset			
Are you generally positive and motivated?			
General wellbeing			
Are you generally healthy and strong?			

Total score (add up all your points): _____

What does your points total say about your health?

Now take your points total from the health checklist and read the section that corresponds to your score.

0–5 points

A lack of health can impact every part of your life, as everyone with this score will be aware. A low score may be due to a chronic or major health issue, or the effects of an unhealthy lifestyle. It's time to look at your life and choose to create habits that will give you the physical strength and health you need to create life-changing goals and fulfil your dreams.

Here are some tips for taking control of your health and wellbeing.

1   *Listen to your body.* Your body usually gives you signals when things are not optimal or if you have some sort of deficiency. So pay attention to the way you feel. Cravings, light-headedness, tiredness, grumpiness, headaches and fogginess are all readily apparent symptoms, as are aches and pains. If you're not in tip-top shape, look at yourself to see what is missing: is it regular/adequate nourishment, sleep or exercise, or are you suffering excess stress? Physical symptoms should not be ignored, especially when they continue for more than a few weeks. Burying your head in the sand will not make them go away. Learn to listen to your body and do what's right for your body first — before anything else. Your body should be your number-one priority, because without your health life can be a struggle.

2   *Be an informed eater.* The better educated you are about health and nutrition, the healthier your daily decisions are likely to be. Learn about the nutrition your body needs to function well and what foods provide

(continued)

What does your points total say about your health? (cont'd)

that nutrition. Learn the difference between good and bad fats. Understand why you need more vegetables, what processed food contains and why fast food is so addictive. Read the ingredient labels on food before you buy it, and if you are unsure of what something is, google it. You are much more likely to make a healthy choice if you understand what your choices are.

3 *Get active.* Explore different kinds of exercise so that you can find something that suits your body and lifestyle. Many unfit people equate fitness with gyms, running and pain. But fitness can be fun for everyone! Take an hour each day to play outdoors with your kids, walk to work while listening to your favourite music and, if you are really up for an adventure, take lessons in flying trapeze.

4 *Make time to look after yourself.* Most people feel they don't have enough time in the day to get everything done, which is why fast food is so attractive and exercise often gets skipped. Schedule time in your diary for eating well, exercising and otherwise taking care of yourself, including sufficient time to enjoy yourself and rest. Apparently, it takes 21 days to create a new habit. Spend the next three weeks creating a new life habit where your health comes first.

5 *Cook more.* Understanding how to cook delicious, healthy food means you are far more likely to eat it. If you can't cook, or you tend to cook greasy, stodgy or otherwise unhealthy meals, find someone to teach you their favourite healthy recipes. There are also thousands of great recipes on the internet. Find a healthy ingredient that you have not cooked with before—such as quinoa, beetroot or spinach—and try a delicious, new recipe that includes that ingredient.

6–10 points

Your health is pretty good but you know you have some room for improvement. Perhaps you are generally healthy but lacking in fitness. Perhaps you have a condition that holds you back sometimes. Whatever your experience of health and fitness, now is the time when a few small lifestyle changes can make a big difference to your long-term health.

If you are one of the countless people who are too busy to exercise, then choose to prioritise it in your life. You are responsible for your health and wellbeing and the difference between fit people and unfit people is exercise! Choose a new healthy habit that will get you sweating a few times a week. Find something you will enjoy doing and you will be much more likely to stick with it.

11–16 points

You are in tip-top health! Considering your score, you probably look after yourself and are doing all the right things. You appreciate that it feels good to feel good, so you think about what you eat and get active on a regular basis. If you are young, don't take it for granted! Develop and keep good habits throughout your life and you may live longer, look younger and feel better than many people your age.

How does your lifestyle score?

You can now see how your lifestyle scores in many important areas. Use the scores to give you an overall impression of what is working and not working in your life right now. Are there areas you have sacrificed or forgotten? Are there areas where a few simple changes could make a big difference to your quality of life?

Use the scores as a benchmark for your life right now and then come back and do the checklists again in six months' time. Take some time to appreciate what you have in your life and then focus on the areas where you would like to make a change.

Notice how your score changes when you are working on a life-changing project. Notice how much changes from year to year. We are often so wrapped up in our daily lives that we lose sight of what we have accomplished along the way.

What have you been dreaming of?

I have a huge number of dreams, interests and things I want to do in my life. In the past I had a habit of taking action towards achieving some of them, but kept putting off the big ones until next year or the year after, when I believed I would have more time. One of my big goals was to travel through Latin America for six months.

The problem with this goal was that next year never came. When I was working for someone else this seemed like a valid excuse. I was an account manager, so my targets were all designed a year in advance. In order to take six months off I would have had to quit my well-paid job and hope to find another on my return.

The prospect of how hard that might be knocked my confidence, so I deferred and deferred.

Then in 2006 I quit my job (and my income) and tried my luck creating my own business and other social endeavours. I went from working five days a week for a big income to working six or seven days a week for very little income.

It took me a while to figure out what I wanted to do, and the debts started to pile up. Despite this change to my lifestyle, my trip was still a year or two away — still just a conversation and a daydream. And that was all.

Looking back, I can see that although I talked about the trip all the time, I never started the process of going. I never looked at the price of airline tickets or calculated how much money I would need to save. I never bought a guidebook or followed travel blogs. I never set a date. All of these inactions gave me the big fat result of nothing.

Does this sound familiar? Do you have an unfulfilled dream? Is there something you always have far out in the future that you 'should' or 'would' do if there were not a whole lot of reasons why you can't?

A million reasons why not

Some of you will have very valid reasons why you can't pursue your dream — very, very valid reasons. The more valid they are, the more you will be held back because they are easy to believe — they justify your status quo and keep you doing the same things over and over.

In 2009 I met my husband-to-be and one of the first things I told him was about my 'plan' to spend six months in Latin America. He had always wanted to go too, so we were happy in our little shared dream for another year, and then another year.

One day I cracked. We walked past a travel agency and I just couldn't ignore my dream any longer, so we went in to enquire about costs.

Of course, to get a quote for flights, you need dates …

At this point I had a reality check. If we didn't set a date for travel we would never go. There would always be a reason why it is inconvenient. John (my husband) loved his job. I was actively paying off debts and my business was starting to do well. I was having a lot of fun growing it and I needed to be there for the promotion of my first book. We loved where we lived, we were surrounded by great friends and for the first time everything was going right for us both. There were many very good reasons why we shouldn't leave to travel, why it was impossible for us to leave and still make the most of what we had created.

The problem was that if we waited a couple of years we were likely to have kids, buy a house, and get a dog, some fish and a lawnmower — and the trip would be impossible then too.

So we bought the tickets.

Fast-forward to now and we have leisurely worked our way up from Australia and New Zealand to Venezuela and Colombia, right through Central America and Mexico, and I am writing this chapter on a rooftop overlooking the turquoise ocean in a gorgeous town in the south of Cuba.

Our return ticket has long since been forgotten and we are blowing in the wind of a lifestyle we have designed for ourselves.

Action: list your past and current reasons/excuses

Write a list of all your unfulfilled dreams and all the reasons and excuses you have for not making them a reality. Include all your dreams, large and small. Now look at the most common reasons/excuses you have for not fulfilling your dreams.

My unfulfilled dreams	My reasons for why I am yet to make this happen
Learn to play the guitar	I am too old to learn and I am too busy to practise...
Travel the world	I don't have enough money and we have children and many other commitments and responsibilities...

Be an Action Taker

It appears that there are some people in the world who are less inhibited about taking action on the things they are passionate about than others — let's call them Action Takers.

Apparently I am one of them! The only difference between an Action Taker and someone who does not take action, is taking action.

Action Takers don't have any super powers, or special DNA (that I know of!); they are simply willing to get talking, get into action and risk failure in the bid to realise their dreams.

The size of the dreams you dare to chase is exactly in proportion to the size of your willingness to risk failure.

In other words, if you allow yourself the possibility of encountering a big failure, it means you are willing to pursue bigger dreams; and every once in a while, the momentum you build taking action to realise those dreams is enough to completely alter your life.

Action Takers take action over and over again until life begins to resemble what they have been hoping for and dreaming about. Their determination to achieve their goals means they will persist, even if they fail big sometimes and even if they have no idea how to achieve what they want to achieve.

Time and time again, people come to me for coaching after years of daydreaming, settling for their valid excuses or procrastinating. Then, during their first big project, they find their feet and are off at 100 miles an hour: they realise that their life is just waiting for them to get started. Their perception of life often completely alters in a matter of months, simply because they are taking action.

In each chapter we will look at actions you can take to get where you want to go and resources to help you along the way. Take action and you will become someone who thinks and then does, someone who has an idea and then starts the process of creation without worrying about all the reasons why you can't do it.

The bucket list

A bucket list is a list of all the things you want to do or have before you kick the bucket (die).

Having a list like this can provide you with a rough guide for the direction of your life. It shows which adventures you would like to have and what you would like to achieve. It can change often, as you cross things off and add new things that take your fancy.

There are no right things for your bucket list; it is *your* list of the things *you* want to achieve. Once you achieve an item on the list, put a line through it and look for what's next!

In 2012 I started a bucket list. The full list has about forty-five goals written on it now. Here are the first 20.

Goal	Status
1 Learn to sail — sail the world	No plans as yet.
2 Learn guitar and get good!	Started to learn, but no room for a guitar on our travels.
3 Visit 100 inspiring community projects around the world and share their stories	We have filmed 19 community projects so far, all in Latin America.
4 Visit Machu Picchu	Done! September 2013.
5 Swim with a whale shark	Still trying. I have been close but no luck... yet!
6 Learn to knit or crochet	I would like to learn the next time I am in NZ.
7 Dive the Blue Hole (Belize), explore underwater cities and dive more cenotes in Mexico	Blue Hole: done! No plans yet for underwater cities but I have done some research into several possibilities. I hope Mexico will happen in the next couple of years.
8 Write three best-selling books	One down!

Goal	Status
9 Create a school for young social entrepreneurs	Just a daydream at present.
10 Spend 6 to 12 months each in Latin America, Africa and South-East Asia	18 months in Latin America: done. Rough plans for Africa. Rough plans for Asia.
11 Learn to cook Vietnamese food like a native	Rough plans for next year.
12 Learn permaculture; grow a lush vegetable garden or food forest	Just daydreams right now.
13 Spend time in space	This seems like such a big goal! Still dreaming at this stage.
14 Learn the trapeze	Two lessons so far, on hold while we travel.
15 Live in a small, friendly, coastal community in a Spanish-speaking country, in a wooden house complete with hammocks and a writing room with a view	Still looking for the perfect location. Current favourites are in Mexico, Colombia, Cuba and Ecuador.
16 Fly in a hot-air balloon	It's in the diary for April!
17 Become an excellent photographer	Learning and practising as I go. I would love to do a course too.
18 Go to loads of great international festivals, including Burning Man Festival (USA)	Started in Australasia and then will head to Europe this year. No plans yet for Burning Man.
19 Get fit enough to enter some sort of endurance event and finish!	I like the idea of this more than the reality.
20 Learn how to make cheese	Keen to try recipes and courses next time I am in NZ.

Action: create a bucket list

Now create your own bucket list. Make the list as long as it needs to be. List all the things you dream of having or doing. Add to it any unfulfilled dreams from any previous lists and any new dreams and goals as they arise. For example, you might start with:

Goal	Status
Sail around the world with the family.	Unplanned as yet.

What are your talents?

One day a good friend, Johana, confided that she has always had a dream to sing and has been quietly taking singing lessons. She gave me a flyer and invited me to a concert where some of her teacher's students would sing on stage for the first time to an audience of family and friends.

When I arrived, I was ushered downstairs to a dark, cosy room with big velvet curtains and a stage just big enough to hold a piano, a chair and a microphone. The night started and each singer got up to sing a song or two. It was Johana's turn and she got up, said a few words and started to sing. I can't remember what it was that she sang, but I will never forget my goosebumps as her raw, beautiful voice filled the room. It floored me to see this woman I knew so well share her newly discovered talent with a room of witnesses who'd be able to remind her that it really happened!

I love that moment of recognition and delight when someone blows everyone away — usually including themselves because of the reaction they get. If there is one kind of YouTube clip I love to see, it is the kind where the most unassuming people open their mouths to reveal a most breathtaking singing talent that is overwhelmingly acknowledged by the audience.

Although I am talking about singers, this principle is the same for people with any talent — every person has their own unique talent and potential just dying to be explored and utilised. For singers it may be easy to figure out: they hum along to the radio as kids would and *voilà!* they realise they can sing. For many talents, however, it may not be so clear. Many people do not discover their talent until they have tried many things that they are not talented at. Some people never have the chance to discover what it is.

In my case I believe one of my talents is to help people see that they actually can achieve the things they wish to achieve, step by step. In other words, I enjoy breaking down complicated projects and motivating people to get started and keep going. This, coupled with my experience starting, failing and succeeding in many projects and businesses of my own, means that coaching and writing is the perfect way for me to use my talent. But it took me years of trial and error to figure that out! Without the experiences I had I would never have discovered this as a fulfilling path. If someone had told me as a teenager I should be a business coach or a writer it would have made no sense to me. It was only through actively searching and making the most of the opportunities I sought out that it became apparent. Even then, I needed to have the guts to get started and the persistence to build and maintain momentum.

Of course, there is usually plenty of time in life to discover the dozens of talents you have that could give you a huge sense of joy and fulfilment. They may impact your relationships, career or businesses or the big dreams you long for. Some of your talents will help you achieve those dreams and some of your talents may only become apparent after you have succeeded or failed at something you have worked very hard for. But the result will enable you to take the next step in discovering what else you can achieve in this world.

Chapter 3

Goals and success

Think for a moment about people you have heard of who have achieved great things.

Regardless of whether they are inventors, athletes, activists, musicians, or founders of businesses or charity projects, they all have one thing in common: they had a big goal and they performed a series of actions to reach it.

What is your attitude to goals?

The thought of setting goals creates different feelings for different people, as do our interpretations of success. We are now going to look at your attitude to goal-setting and your interpretation of success and then create a common foundation for both that we can use throughout the book.

Creating goals

The first step to great success is creating great goals.

Now, having a big goal does not mean that it will turn out the way you think. But it is the critical first step, because it enables you to know what you are aiming for. Your goals will define the actions you need to take, so we can safely say that goals are essential! Before we create any, let's consider your attitude to goals.

Some people create goals on a regular basis, while others are careful about what they hope and dream for. Some revere their goals, while others let them slip and slide.

Some people announce their goals to the world; others work at them quietly and announce them when they have already had some success.

Some people create a new goal every week; others have the same ones throughout their lives. Some will be too afraid to have any goals at all.

What type of person have you been until now?

Are you ready for life-changing goals?

Undergoing a big life change is a two-part process:

⇨ The moment when it all changes in your head.

⇨ The moment when it all changes in your world.

The moment when it all changes in your head

This is the shift in your mindset that motivates you to take new actions. It could be caused by many things, including:

⇨ a health scare

⇨ the death of a loved one

⇨ the loss of a job

⇨ losing your tolerance for a certain job or boss

⇨ having your first child

⇨ an inspiring conversation

⇨ a Good Life Crisis (see chapter 1).

We'll talk more about this later but, in short, something happens that makes you re-evaluate your life, your belief in yourself and your future. It could be any event, big or small, but once it happens the wheels are set in motion ... you find yourself looking for new opportunities, considering your options, taking risks that you had dismissed in the past, dreaming about what could be, and taking the steps you need to get to where you want to be.

In this phase you may change careers, start a new business, find a new relationship, look at how you can create income from a hobby, ask for help, create a plan, start volunteering, campaign for a cause, book a course, travel or start something you have spent years dreaming of.

This phase is driven by what is *possible* rather than what *is*. For example:

⇨ You may or may not have support for your ideas and life change.

⇨ You may or may not have the time or finances to transition easily.

⇨ You may or may not have the experience you need to make things work.

⇨ You may or may not have a plan.

⇨ You will potentially need to manage naysayers, fear or uncertainty; risks; and the fact that you will fail at some things along the way.

But at this point, anything is possible and you need to keep putting one foot in front of the other and move towards your goal.

This is the part where, if you persevere, you will experience a strength that you never knew you had; a work ethic that will make the impossible, possible; a resilience that makes no risk too scary; and a passion for life that radiates from your every cell.

Fortunately, not all of us experience the tragedy or jarring challenges that are often the catalyst for shaking our 'anything is possible' mindset into life. Unfortunately, this mindset does not come naturally to many of us.

We are trained to believe that failure is a thing to be avoided at all costs. We are encouraged to strive to be the best, but within the confines of the system. The game is set; it is bad to break the rules and even risky to be too innovative. We are conditioned to work hard, do what we are told, respect the authorities and learn what we are supposed to learn.

It doesn't matter whether you want to lose weight, learn a new instrument, fight for a cause or start a business. If it is something you have no experience in (or in which you have only experienced failure), it is a mental challenge that could require you to completely transform or renew your values, mindset and self-belief in order to succeed.

The moment when it all changes in your world

This is the bit where all the hard work, the belief, the optimism and the intensity pay off and the momentum you create starts to affect the world around you. It is the moment when you realise that you are making a profit, creating a buzz, getting a book deal, or crossing the finish line of your first half-marathon.

When your world starts to resemble your plan, the experience is electric! Not only do you feel a surging sense of accomplishment, but often other exciting opportunities start to arise around you. You become a magnet for other people who are following their dreams. You will notice fluidity in finding the resources you need to make things happen. You become more comfortable with making bigger goals and having more exciting dreams. And along the way, you will notice your opinion of yourself start to change.

You will begin to see failure as a part of the process and not something to be feared or endured with shame. You will start to feel confident in your ability to create the world around you, and confident that you can impact things and make a difference to the things that are important to you.

In my experience this creates more and more moments of peace, fulfilment and intense joy.

During this journey there are a few questions you need to ask yourself that will guide the direction you take:

➩ What is important to you?

➩ How important is it to you?

➩ How have you been behaving about it until now? (Like, *really!*)

➩ What do you want?

➩ When do you want it?

➩ What are you willing to sacrifice for it?

This is where I introduce you to Mark, who found himself asking these questions, with life-changing results.

 Case study: acquiring a tropical island with no money

Mark Bowness's life was over. He was 26 when his marriage ended, he lost his job, had no money, and moved back in with his parents.

When he woke up in a hospital bed after attempting to end his life, Mark realised he had a second chance. He chose to look at what he wanted in life, rather than at the little he had at that moment.

While dreaming about islands, beaches and sunsets he wanted to see if he could make that kind of life a reality.

Challenge 1: acquire a tropical island with no money.

Mark quickly got into action. He found Ben, who had some experience building in remote places, and asked if he could create a partnership with him. He started to call owners of private islands in different places and learned what he could

---

(continued)

Case study: acquiring a tropical island with no money *(cont'd)*

about island ownership. During one call he found out that in Fiji you can't buy islands, but you can lease them. Suddenly the dream became much more affordable.

Mark and Ben went to Fiji to speak with the chief of an island. Mark wanted to bring a tribe of people in to develop ecotourism there, which would benefit the locals. As luck would have it, the chief had a similar vision and the lease was agreed upon. Tribe Wanted was born.

Mark and Ben went on to build a tribe and a documentary series, and to achieve many of their goals in Fiji.

The confidence he got from this project made Mark realise that he could design his life according to his own personal values, and he now lives an adventurous and fulfilling life helping others to see their potential via his website. See **www.lifechangetherevolution.com**

The thing about success

The concept of success is completely subjective. Many of us strive for success that emulates our perception of other people's success. But this is often a superficial slice of reality — a temporary illusion!

Who is successful to you? What does success mean? Why is it so important?

I am a best-selling author. Does that make me any more special than someone who writes for themselves at home? No, it doesn't! Do you think this label affects how I live my life? No. At the end of the day, I still brush my teeth, do the dishes and go to bed like everyone else.

I love that people achieve great things and it inspires me to know that *it is possible* to achieve great things. But even great achievers just see life as normal! It doesn't matter who you are; you need to sleep, eat, connect with people and try new things. It doesn't matter who you are or what you have achieved in the past; it is what you achieve today that matters. It is what you are striving for that matters more than any past success.

Success opens the door to more opportunities, but the benefits are often short-lived, because even with success you need to be striving for the next dream or goal in order to feel alive and be making the most of your life.

Life levels the playing field: you can achieve great things, just like everyone else. If you are someone who spends a lot of time dreaming about success, make sure you are also actively working on achieving that success.

Are you prepared to fail?

Until you put yourself in a position where you risk big failure, it is hard to know how you will deal with it when it happens or when you think it may be happening.

When people think they are failing, it is not uncommon for them to experience feelings of panic, stress, self-doubt and anger and/or to appear crazy, frantic or completely nuts.

When people think they have failed, it is not uncommon for them to experience guilt, disappointment, anger, humiliation, self-doubt, blame and even depression.

Let's face it, failure sucks! Especially when you are trying to achieve something really important to you, or when other people are relying on your success. The bigger the goals you attempt to achieve, the more you risk and the more intense the experience is if you think you are going to — or actually do — fail.

Sometimes impending failure is worse than failure itself and it can cause people to make desperate decisions and act impulsively.

If you have spent your life inside the confines of safety, or are used to winning and being the best, I suggest you decide now what your attitude to failure is going to be. Choose a saying you will repeat to yourself when things are not going your way. Choose something that will remind you that failure is a normal part of the 'fulfilling your dreams' process. You may fail and you may not fail, and if you do fail it will just be part of your ultimate success story.

For me the reminder is 'failure is a step on the path to success'. It helps me to remember that any current situation, however awful, is only temporary.

The risky road

Starting a life-changing project generally requires you to take some real or perceived risks that you may normally avoid taking. As I've said, risk is something that many people run a mile from, especially if they can see that there are many possible things that could go wrong.

In addition to failing, you risk plenty of other things, including:

➪ losing the time or money you invest in your project

➪ being judged at every step of the journey

➪ making life harder for yourself

➪ not being able to do what you want to do

➪ seeing your dreams in the harsh light of reality

➪ alienating people who may not support your changing ideas and goals

➪ being seen as a failure by people who are important to you.

If you find you are naturally risk-averse, dig deeper and understand what it is you are afraid of. It is important to analyse these feelings rather than just behave as you automatically have in the past, because this time you are looking for new kinds of results and a change in life. This means you need to change how you perceive risk.

To create any great thing in life, you have to put something at risk. Risk is a good thing for many reasons, because it separates those who *dream* from those who *do*. Being a doer in a conditioned world of dreamers makes you stand out, which can significantly help your project.

With an element of risk, most people will plan more carefully. There is a balancing act between being creative in mitigating risk and being willing to take great risk when the time is right. Some people are born with this instinct. If luck is on their side and they have judged it right, they may become an overnight success story. Someone else may not be so lucky and may experience great failure in their first big project. Luckily there is usually another chance — if they don't give up after the first, second or fifth attempt, that is.

Some people deal with their aversion to risk by deliberately taking small steps in the quest for their goal. There is nothing wrong with this, but it will be a long road to life-changing results. Over time, as they see small successes from small goals, they may muster up the courage to risk making bigger goals that carry greater risks.

Don't be down on your goal

You have the opportunity to change the world, create wealth, travel long-term or have any of your other dreams come true, just like everyone else on this planet.

If you are not already on the path to making your big dreams happen there is probably some sort of conversation in your head that is persuading you otherwise. My advice is to stop listening to it!

If you are to make your dream come true you need to be the person who has the most belief in it. There is no time or place for you to be down on your project. It will likely be hard enough anyway without your negative and discouraging thoughts.

If you truly want change in your life, you will have to be responsible for your thoughts and feelings, as they are potentially the only things standing in your way! So notice when you have negative thoughts, and catch yourself saying anything to the detriment of your goal. If you are your own worst critic, then you need to silence that critic and bring in some other more supportive and positive voices.

If you're someone prone to doubting yourself, give yourself a positive mental shake-up! First, catch yourself in the act. You may be so used to the negative self-talk that you don't even notice it whispering away in your head.

The thing to realise about the negative voice in your head is that if you are listening to it, it is no longer you! It is separate from you. So get into the habit of noticing the voice there, rather than automatically assuming the voice is your own.

You can aid the process of distinguishing *you* from the incessant ramblings in your head with meditation, personal development or any other practice that helps you calm your thoughts and be present in the current moment.

When I notice that my mind is running wild with stress, overwhelm or other negative thoughts, I take a deep breath and focus on how the air feels in my chest, how it feels as it flows in and out, and how my ribs rise and fall.

This clears my head and allows me to focus on what is happening right now (breathing) as opposed to everything else that could possibly go wrong. For me this 30-second meditation is enough to bring down my stress levels, slow my heart rate and help me see genuine options as opposed to stress, panic or overwhelm. The majority of bad things that we anticipate never happen, yet we waste so much time running them through our minds.

If the only thing you did in the next 12 months was learn to calm your mind, that alone may have a life-changing effect and increase your chances of success.

Chapter 4

Make the impossible, possible

What can you create? Is your dream possible? Do you want something that is impossible?

Imagine a world where anything was possible if a) you put your mind to it, and b) you took all the actions necessary to make it happen. Imagine a world where you could have a big dream that you have no idea how to fulfil and you could go out there and fulfil it. Imagine a world where you could take something you are very passionate about and make a whole career out of it, a world where you could completely alter your life in just 12 months.

Well, the good news is that you already live in this world. The bad news is that making the impossible, possible takes a big commitment and often a lot of work. The great news is that if you spend your life striving for big, exciting goals, you will reach some of them and in doing so you are in fact designing and creating your life.

Case study: how to be a farmer when you don't have a farm

When Andrew Hearne was 12 he knew he wanted to be a farmer. His declaration was met with laughter from his family and the message was clear: he would never have enough money to buy a farm.

He took a mainstream path but after a decade in a corporate job, the call of the earth was too great and he took on a lawn-mowing franchise so that he could pay the bills while he went back to study horticulture and landscape design. Andrew took courses for seven years as he grew his business to incorporate all he was learning.

Andrew was 45 when his marriage broke down, he moved to the city and took a job as a commercial landscaper. One day he was at a seminar and the presenter shouted at the audience to 'eat organic food'! At that moment Andrew decided he would follow his lifelong dream to become a farmer.

He sprang into action.

Challenge 1: buy and set up a farm with no capital.

While Andrew started to look for suitable farms he also spoke to everyone he could about his dream. In the process he fell in love with Therese, who had a similar dream of growing organic food. Together they met another couple who shared their passion, and a plan was made.

Therese owned an apartment and the bank agreed to give them a 95-per-cent loan against it for the farm. Eighteen months after he decided to chase the dream, they moved to their new land and business: Near River Produce.

At first things were tough. They had no money for infrastructure—no irrigation, no tractor—and for two years they mowed the lawns with a push mower. Without equipment, and determined not to use chemicals, they had to prepare each growing bed by hand.

The local farming community thought they were nuts and suggested it would be much easier to use the chemicals first to clear the fields and then apply for organic status afterwards. However, they stuck to their ideals, worked it manually and two months later their first beds were ready for planting.

Meanwhile they bought seven laying hens and fed them organic food. Although Andrew and Therese had no experience with chickens, the hens started laying super healthy eggs.

The farm has gone from strength to strength. Andrew and Therese thrive on the positive feedback they get from customers and they educate the community about the importance of healthy food. The demand for their eggs means they now have hundreds of hens and work with a neighbouring farm, which also keeps to their strict organic practices.

As for the locals in the community who once shook their heads, many have confided how proud they are that they stuck to their guns and farmed the old- fashioned way. See **www.nearriverproduce.com**

Is *anything* possible ... like, really?

For many of us our big goals and dreams fall into a category of things that we may not even consider possible. This is because the change that needs to occur is so big that we can't see the path to realising success. Our goal may need more funds than we can imagine ourselves ever having access to. Our work or family situation may present unsurmountable challenges. The reality is that certain dreams actually are impossible, aren't they?

When it comes to achieving enormous, challenging goals, you will find plenty of opinions about whether your goal is possible or impossible — many of them will be your own opinions or those of people who are important to you. So how do you define what actually is possible? Are some of your goals possible and some impossible? Is it beneficial to be practical when you are choosing your goals?

Can you really sail the world for a year with your kids? Can you really start a more fulfilling career when you have no experience, and bills to pay? Can you really change your country's attitudes to child welfare, animal welfare or the environment when you have no clue how to navigate politics? Can you really publish a bestseller when you've never written a book before, start your property portfolio when you have no capital, or fall in love with the person of your dreams when you have failed relationships haunting you? Can you really start a successful business?

The answer to all these seemingly impossible questions and millions more just like them, is *yes!* (I know this because I have heard of or met people who have done all of these things.)

It is possible for you to choose a goal that is seemingly impossible and make the impossible, possible. You probably read about people who do incredible things every day. You probably know people who have fought against all odds to achieve their goals.

Now — today — at this very moment, it is time for that person to be you.

Building the 'anything is possible' habit

You will often hear that anything is possible and most of the time I believe this to be true … anything *is* possible!

Some people are born with an inherent belief that anything is possible. Those people tend to start out young, experimenting with new ideas, projects, adventures and businesses. They constantly push the boundaries. They are often the people who achieve great things relatively early in life and continue doing so throughout their lives.

They are naturally in the habit of believing that anything is possible.

For everyone else, there is the opportunity to build this fantastic habit. You too can be someone who approaches all challenges optimistically and with a sense of adventure. You too can create outrageous goals and then do whatever it takes to achieve them.

As I mentioned earlier, your mindset defines your ability to reach your goals, and your belief that anything is possible is crucial to overcoming seemingly impossible obstacles.

Start to notice when you have doubts in your abilities. You need to be able to nip that unhelpful habit in the bud to be able to push through the hard bits.

There are occasions when I catch myself not believing anything is possible. It usually happens when I've created a massive goal or when I've failed at something. To snap myself out of it, I ask myself, 'If anything is possible then what will I do next to create what I want?' This changes my thinking from 'I can't' to 'How can I?' and I usually find there is a solution I hadn't seen before.

Case study: believing in yourself even when you have no experience

Susanna Davidov was a graphic-design student who loved fashion and travelling. People would comment on the unique artisanal pieces she wore, so when she travelled, she started buying extras for her friends at home. One day she decided to create a business importing quality artisanal products from around the world. She wanted to share the stories of the artisans and help keep their traditions alive. She wanted to do this by using her profits to support charities and projects that would benefit the artisans in some way.

Susanna entered a few funding competitions at university and found herself up against business students, but her passion made up for her lack of business training and she succeeded! The funding enabled her to buy a number of products and a website domain name…and SunChild Collective was born!

Faced with many people who didn't believe in her abilities, she pressed on and learned to run the business through trial and error, working every night and weekend. She turned down a couple of great job opportunities even though she had no idea if her business would work out.

Despite the ups and downs, within a year Susanna made the business profitable. She has been contacted by some major chains keen to stock her products and is already helping the artisans she buys from to improve their lives and keep their traditional crafts alive.

With the economic downtown in the United States, many of her fellow students found themselves without work, and a few have since interned for Susanna to get the experience they need for their résumés. When you start a project you never quite know how things will turn out, especially when you don't have experience. In Susanna's case, she was able to create something beautiful that looked impossible in other people's eyes. See **www.sunchildcollective.com**

How to make the impossible, possible

So how do you make the impossible, possible? How do you change your mindset so dramatically that you can do things you seemingly couldn't do before? The answer is *one step at a time*. You have been cultivating your current mindset all your life, and although it is possible to change your mindset overnight, for most of us it takes practice and some time to adjust.

If you are really committed, changing your mindset can come lightning fast. If you are cynical, resigned and lacking drive, it can occur really slowly or not at all. Change is your choice, even if you don't feel like it is.

As I said in chapter 2, a change in your mindset may come from a variety of situations and experiences. You can also develop your mindset by being inspired by courses, books, new friends, associates and mentors, as well as taking on new adventures and seemingly impossible or big goals.

It's easy to stay stuck in your ways when you have nothing at stake or nothing huge you really want to progress towards. Conversely, it can be difficult to stay stuck in your ways when you can see the real possibility of your dreams coming true.

Making the impossible, possible is not rocket science; it is about becoming someone who looks for the solutions to all that stands in the way of making your dreams come true and leaving behind the part of you that says you can't have anything and everything you want out of life.

Chapter 5

Design your life

Now that we've covered everything that's likely to be going on in your head, we've arrived at the *doing* part of the book. This is where you start to think out loud and commit your dreams to paper; create tangible goals; and plan the actions you need to take in order to make it all happen.

The first step is to decide what results you want your actions to give you. If you were living a life you had designed, what would it look like? If this is not something you daydream about, spend some time doing so. Let your imagination run wild.

- ✏ Who would you be?
- ✏ Where would you go?
- ✏ What would you do?
- ✏ Where would you live?
- ✏ Who would you live and/or spend time with?
- ✏ Who would you help?

☞ What would give you fulfilment and joy?

☞ What would you want to create?

☞ What legacy would you like to leave?

This is possibly the most important step in the process. The vision of what your dream life looks like and how much that excites and inspires you is what will get and keep you moving towards your goal until you reach it (or a version of it that you're thrilled with).

This bit can be really fun, but it may also be confronting. Many people are uncomfortable creating a vision or goals without knowing how they will achieve them.

Note: If the goal you create in this next step does not strike some fear in your belly then your goal is probably too small to be life-changing. If this is you, think bigger!

There is of course nothing wrong with creating small goals, but if it's a fundamental life change you're after, you'll need to create big, ground-shaking goals. So it is time to think big.

It's important to note that it is an inherent trait of our human nature to play safe and aim for the things we know we will succeed at; in other words, to create small goals. The problem is that the resulting change in your life will directly correlate with the size of the goals you have created and the actions you take to fulfil them. To change your life, you need to create life-changing goals.

If you make achievable goals and take the actions required to achieve them, you will have a nice, safe and achievable life — probably the life you have right now.

If you make seemingly unachievable or far-reaching, life-changing goals and take the actions required to achieve them, you will change your life significantly.

You can have your achievable goals too, of course, but it is life-changing goals that we focus on in this book ... so here we go!

Create life-changing goals

Life-changing goals are goals that are likely to change your life, whether you succeed or fail in the process. These goals are thrilling, but usually come with a lot of uncertainty because there is a lot to learn, there is a lot riding on the outcome (your dream life!), you may have no idea if you can generate the resources you need and you may risk many things that you would normally avoid risking.

Five Point Five: our life-changing goal

When my husband John and I booked our tickets to Venezuela, we gave ourselves four months to get organised and pack up our lives in Australia. We had a one-year return ticket that we could alter to fit our journey if needed.

Aside from the logistical and financial planning, we started to ask ourselves, 'What if we could do something that had meaning while we travelled? Rather than just travel for fun, what if we could use it to make a positive difference to others in some way?'

We considered different charities we could work with as well as volunteering opportunities. We started to talk to people about the ideas we had. We wanted our trip to have some meaning, so we started to build the idea, including working up a few different concepts.

After much brainstorming, we settled on a life-changing goal to travel the world making mini-documentaries about people who make a difference to their communities.

Before embarking on a project such as Five Point Five, most people would ask themselves a number of questions, such as:

➪ Do we know how to produce mini-documentaries?

➪ Do we have the equipment to film them?

➪ Do we understand the editing process?

➪ Do we know how to find the people we will film?

➪ Do we speak Spanish?

➪ Do we have enough time to start a whole new project from scratch?

➪ Do we have the capital to build this the way we envision?

For most people, if the answer is 'no' to any or some of these questions, the show would be over before it starts. For them it would seem impossible.

We answered 'no' to every question, but as you will notice throughout this book, we laugh in the face of impossibility! We overcome limitations by turning them into opportunities — by using creativity and persistence and giving ourselves permission to dream big.

So the big questions are, 'Do you give yourself permission to create a life-altering goal and then take action to achieve it? Are you willing to look at limitations as challenges and opportunities on the path to your potential success?'

If the answers are 'yes', let's proceed ... it's time to design your life!

Action: create a life-changing goal

Return to your bucket list (see chapter 2) and add anything else that you have thought of since you wrote it. Now include the things you have given yourself permission to dream about since reading this chapter of the book.

Look at your list and choose one item that is the most exciting to you: the thing you would really like to work on the most. We'll start with this first and use it as the project to work on throughout the remainder of the book.

Remember, this is not the time to be thinking about all the reasons why you can't, won't and shouldn't choose a specific goal. This is where you choose the goal you want most in the world, regardless of any considerations or possible limitations. The bigger the goal, the bigger the resulting outcome for your life. So pick the most exciting goal — the one that, if you fulfilled it, would change the way you live your life. For example:

Goal: to sail the world with the family for one year.

Set a time frame

This is the important bit. Without a time frame your goal is likely to slip into sometime/never land.

Your goal should have a clear date when it will be achieved or fulfilled. Preferably this should be sooner rather than later. If you are unsure of how long it will take, start with an arbitrary time frame such as three months or, if it is a huge project, 12 months. You can revise your goal at the end of that time, but if you aim high in a short space of time you will be surprised how much you can accomplish.

If your goal is something that will definitely be more than 12 months in the making (such as, for example, publishing a series of books or setting up a charity) then set yourself a 12-month goal that will be an exciting and significant milestone towards achieving your big goal.

Five Point Five: our 12-month goal

When we started, our initial 12-month goals were:

- to travel through Latin America and build a great website with sponsors, quality partnerships and an active and growing community

- to travel, meet inspiring people and produce a new mini-documentary every month.

If your goal is to travel the world, your 12-month goal could be that you have booked your tickets, saved or made the money to go, and departed your home country; or that you have created an alternative source of income that you can earn while you travel (like we did!).

Action: add a date for achieving your goal

Be specific about the day, month and year of completion of your goal:

> *Goal: to sail the world with the family for one year.*

> *When: we will leave our port by 20 December of this year.*

Create milestones

Milestones are mini-goals that will help keep you on track. They are important: without them you will not be able to objectively assess whether you are on track to achieve what you set out to do.

If you have allowed three months to achieve your goal, set milestones for the end of months 1 and 2.

If you have 12 months to reach your goal, then set milestones for the first three, six and nine months. That way, you know what to focus on at any given time and you can track your progress as you go. In creating milestones, it's important that they are also specific and measurable so you know you have achieved them.

Five Point Five: our milestones

By month 3:

- Secure two partners.
- Secure two sponsors.
- Acquire all the gear we need, ready for filming.

By month 6:

- Find a production team or learn how to use a film editing program.
- Learn about filming stories so we feel confident we know what to do.
- Film our first video.
- Launch the first version of the website.

By month 9:

- Release the first video.
- Be filming one project a month.
- Have three volunteer writers and an editor join the team.

By month 12:

- Release our first e-book.
- Email our database regularly with updates.
- Design the next stages of the website.

As you can see, although there are a million tasks associated with what we have set out to achieve, we have very clear milestones that we are aiming to achieve along the way to our 12-month goal.

Action: add milestones to your goal

The more effective you are in tracking your progress towards your goal and milestones, the more likely you are to reach them. So, don't put your goal and milestones in a drawer. Have a copy in a prominent place where you will see them often.

This is what the milestones for a project of sailing around the world might look like.

Milestones	By when
Create a detailed plan and budget for the journey. Finalise the ocean conservation message we intend to share as a result of the trip.	20 March
Start a website and blog weekly to share our progress. Get a boat licence and any other licences or certification we need.	20 June
Confirm we have enough sponsors and/or crowd funding and/or fundraising and/or savings for a boat, equipment and provisions.	20 September
Hold a final farewell fundraising event. Finalise a food plan. Ensure the whole family has confidence and experience with CPR, life-saving skills and boat maintenance.	20 December

Crucial elements

Now we will look at the crucial elements of your project.

The crucial elements are the things that are essential for you to achieve each of your milestones and therefore your goal. It is important that you define them, because when you are starting a new project (especially something life-changing) you can get so involved in the minutiae that it is easy to forget the big picture and lose focus on what you need and what it is all likely to cost.

> **Five Point Five: our crucial elements**
>
> The crucial elements for us were:
>
> - film and sound gear, laptop and video editing software
> - the ability to reach lots of people (building our community)
> - a place where we could share the videos (website).

Action: add your crucial elements and some key actions for success

If your project was to change a government policy, your crucial elements would include:

☞ knowledge of the political system and how changes are made

☞ thinking of a viable solution to a problem

☞ having a way to appeal to large numbers of people for their support by adding their name to a petition (for example, money, partnership or sponsorship).

If your project was to sail the world with your family for a year, your crucial elements would include:

☞ a sailboat

☞ knowledge of how to maintain every part of the boat

☞ food and consumables for a year (money or sponsorship).

If you were going with the sailing project, for example, beneath your goals and milestones you would make a list of the things you need to do and/or get to achieve each of the crucial elements. This is where you create the steps and actions that will help you fulfil your goal. Your list might begin like this.

Crucial elements	Actions for success
Sailboat	Find someone who wants to swap our house for a boat for one year.
	Get sponsorship/partnership from interested organisations.
	Fundraise, crowdfund, or make or save the money to buy a boat.
	Sell the car and use the money to buy a boat.
Boat-maintenance skills	Volunteer or get a job at a boat repair workshop for experience and knowledge.
Resources for food and consumables for one year	Contact people who sail long-term for their practical tips on planning food.
	Sell our stuff and make more money.
	Get sponsorship for certain elements required.

What you have, what you need and the universe in-between

Most people do not pursue their dreams because they can't see how it would be possible with the resources they have access to — namely, time, money, people, knowledge and experience. For many, creating life-changing goals is so confronting that they avoid doing it altogether. It can be very confronting to have big goals when you have no idea how you will access the resources you need to achieve them. If you are someone who has always struggled financially or who has a very full life already, you may even see the resources required as an insurmountable challenge ... impossible, even.

If you have got to this point but you have a nagging voice in your head that is telling you that you can't achieve your goals because of a lack of resources, take a deep breath and carry on. Later in the book we are going to look at how you can acquire resources that you don't already have. We will look at how you can find time and money and lead a team of amazing people to fulfil your goal.

Unfortunately there is no fairy godmother; 'the right time' may never arrive — the ducks are too happy with their little 'duck lives' to line up for you.

Fortunately this means that any time is the imperfectly perfect time to get started.

Chapter 6

Take action

The distance between where you are now and where you want to be can be calculated in terms of a series of actions.

There is no amount of theory and postulating, or daydreaming and thinking, that will make your dreams come true. The formula is simple: the more action you take now, the faster you will progress towards making your dreams a reality.

Starting something from nothing

There is a certain responsibility you take on when you decide to create something from nothing. It is your baby and your creation and for some people this is a scary proposition. It may not be natural for you to take a leadership role. It may not be natural for you to take responsibility or risk failure. But here you are ready to do it anyway. Good on you!

How do you deal with the expanse between what you have and what you want? How do you cope with people enquiring about your progress and potentially judging you along the way?

The answer is, *one step at a time.*

The only way to get to where you want to go is to take the steps you can take right now. They may not even be very exciting steps, but if you don't take them, you will be no further along than you are right now. Many of the things you act on will not get you the result you were hoping for or expecting, but that is all part of the game.

As well as being potentially confronting, starting something from nothing is also thrilling! Think of it as a jigsaw puzzle: you have a vision of what the finished picture is going to look like and you are going to add in all the little pieces that will make your vision a reality.

When starting something from nothing, start with a brief for your project as if it were a real, tangible thing. This will help you see the big picture. Let your creative juices flow, visualise your end goal and sketch it out. Your brief should be about one page long and should cover the basics.

The full project may look nothing like your original brief, but it is a starting point. I find the act of taking an idea in my head and creating a brief on paper helps me see the idea as a real possibility rather than a daydream.

In my brief I also include five actions I can take to get the project moving. Some of the actions may include calling people who could be interested in being part of the project, or who may have some experience or contacts that could benefit the project. Fulfilling these initial actions will suddenly place you in a different headspace ... your project has begun!

Case study: growing a global passion for vegetables, one family at a time

Pania Robinson had always had a passion for vegetables and discovered her love for growing them when she was studying nutrition. She realised that she wanted to help people grow their own food, but she didn't know how.

For years she looked for a way of doing this, while learning more and more about it. She tried teaching gardening courses and started a website, but she always felt she needed a piece of land and to earn more money before she could really get started.

Finally tired of waiting for everything to be perfect, Pania sat down one day and wrote down her wildest dreams, even though they didn't seem achievable.

The resulting dream goal was to create an education centre with gardens and cooking facilities. She didn't have the resources to build this, so she started to get creative about how she could do it without money.

Pania realised that her website could be her community hub, and from there could reach out to the community to teach people in their own homes, rented facilities and local community gardens.

Her biggest challenge has always been dealing with her internal thoughts: to stop believing the voice that told her, 'You don't know enough' and 'You are not skilled enough'.

She decided that instead of worrying about what she didn't know, she would focus on the skills and experience she did have. If there were things she needed to know she would learn them along the way or find other people who could help.

With this new mindset Pania brainstormed and mind-mapped all the ideas that were now racing through her head,

(continued)

Case study: growing a global passion for vegetables, one family at a time *(cont'd)*

and then talked them through with friends and a coach to formulate a plan that she could start straight away.

First Pania booked a stand at a local eco-show, which meant she had a date by which her website and plan had to be ready. She then started looking for some families who could be her first students. She contacted a good-news magazine, which was happy to publish her article on the project. She also called some local newspapers and one agreed to run her story straight away.

Several families responded to the articles. For some of them affordable access to more vegetables would mean a dramatic improvement in their diet. Pania started to see that her project was not only needed, but that people were thrilled with the opportunity to learn. Many people from the local community also got in contact, some wanting to help and some wanting to recommend more families in need.

Pania's next step is to find some gardening related sponsors who can help with tools, soil or plants for the families, and she is collating the stories of the families so that sponsors will know exactly who they are helping.

Her big goal is to help people all over the world have access to nourishing food grown in a sustainable way through her project. See **www.joyfulsoil.com**

Actions that can boost your project overnight

As part of any project there are hundreds of actions you could take on any given day, but if you look at your options, some will bring you greater results than others. Here are some actions you can take that will give your project a massive boost — even when you are just starting out!

➯ *Make a list of people worldwide who could advance your project.* They may be people you know or don't know: friends, potential partners, potential sponsors, advisors, mentors, industry experts ... the list is endless. Call someone new each day, or week, and speak to them about your project and what you are aiming to achieve. Gauge interest in any requests or ideas you have, or ask to meet for a coffee if you are in the same city. Network your project. The conversations and connections you make will help give you a pool of fantastic people who can help you with contacts, ideas, their experience and support.

➯ *Make a list of blogs, websites, newspapers, magazines, radio shows and television shows that would be interested in your project.* Write a story about your project and why you are doing it that would appeal to each target media entity. For example, if you are a mum approaching a parenting blog, tell the story from the perspective of a parent. Make sure you tailor the angle of your story to suit each organisation.

➯ *Call each media entity and pitch them the story.* Be prepared to send more information to anyone who is interested.

➯ *Get a coach, friend or partner with whom you can share your progress.* Find someone who would be willing to hold you accountable for achieving your goals. Be in contact with them regularly (weekly or fortnightly) to report on the results of your previous actions and to plan the next ones.

➯ *Post your plans in a public place.* Starting with your social media networks, keep your community posted on your progress and allow them to support you.

> *Choose the thing you think will be the biggest challenge right now.* Then write down 10 different ways you could overcome the challenge.

> *Go to relevant industry events and network your idea.*

> *Find related people or organisations.* Find out who is working in an area related to your project and already has an audience, and form a partnership with them.

These types of actions can give you a big boost of momentum. Here's how we find these tips working for our project, Five Point Five.

Five Point Five: boosting our momentum

The majority of the daily work that needs to be done for Five Point Five is writing blogs, marketing the website through social media, filming and editing videos, and working on the website. These things are creating the foundation on which great things can happen. But the most exciting leaps forward seldom come from these activities alone.

Our biggest jumps in momentum come when outside things happen—such as a newspaper or magazine article or a radio interview—or when a well-known website likes one of our videos and promotes it through its channels.

We tend to get lost in the day-to-day tasks of building our project and forget to make time for the things that will grow us in leaps and bounds. We just work away on what we are doing and every once in a while realise that we need to refocus on what will give us the leaps. At these times we both get out there and contact all the people we can think of who may be interested in our project!

It is during these spurts of focused joint energy that more people join our team, we make ourselves known to new organisations and we find potential partners. To reach our goals we need to intersperse the 'regular work' with these creative and energetic bursts of action that expand our reach.

Any small team (or solo person) attempting to create a big project gets used to the fact that they can't do everything that needs to be done on their own. The pitfall, however, is when you get into the groove of one part of your project and let other important things slide. This is pretty common as most people will do the things they are good at and like doing before they tackle the super-hard things that they have no experience in.

To give yourself the best chance of success, make sure you spread your time between the everyday project development and the bursts of expansion that will grow you exponentially faster.

How to stop procrastinating and get results now

The sun is filtering through enormous French windows onto the bed where I am working. This week we are staying in a beautiful, old, terraced house in Valparaiso, Chile. I have filled the day with sleeping in, cooking meals, researching and writing blog posts, playing with our host's dogs, taking the dogs for a walk, wandering to the shops to buy cakes, posting on social media and other relaxing pastimes.

Unfortunately none of these things will write this chapter for me and so finally, as the day is drawing to an end and while the dogs snooze outside the door, I plump up the pillows, plug in my headphones and settle down to write. Today, I *chose* to do things other than working towards my goal. More often, however, I will start the task I intend to work on and then get distracted and drift away without even realising it. Sometimes it takes me hours to notice!

I know my patterns of procrastination well. They revolve around cups of tea, social media, YouTube videos and everything to do with food and eating. Some of my best work has been created while avoiding what I should have been doing. I am amazed at just how focused I can be when whatever I am doing is not the thing I should be working on.

Procrastination is the way your insecurities sabotage your chances of success. Procrastination is the great leveller. It can turn all great potential to dust.

It doesn't matter how brilliant, talented and skilful you are. What matters is whether you're doing something with your abilities and making the most of the time you have available. Here are some of the things I do to keep the procrastination monster at bay.

Create the right headspace

Starting with the right frame of mind will set you up to be productive and focused. Here are some ways of doing this:

⇨ *Visualise your goal often.* If you lose sight of your goal, the effort you need to achieve each step along the way can start to appear like hard work. Spend some time imagining and creating the moment when your goal is reached. Play it out in your mind: the people, the lifestyle, what you will say when the life you have been dreaming of actually happens.

⇨ *Meditate.* There are many techniques that people use to achieve a meditative state. I learned a basic technique in a short free seminar run by Benjamin J Harvey, founder of Authentic Education in Sydney, and I still use it whenever I wish to get present and clear in my mind. For this technique, I close my eyes but turn them a little to the left and visualise the letter A. I spend a minute or so looking at the A. Then I turn my closed eyes a little to the right and visualise the letter B for a minute or more. Once I have been 'looking' at the letter B for some time I think, 'I am going back to look at the A'. However, instead of doing this I let my (still closed) eyes drift into the middle. The theory is that because I have already focused on the A, my brain believes it already knows the A and therefore doesn't keep thinking about it. This creates a meditative space. It is a simple technique that gives me quiet. The more I practise, the longer I can maintain the silence in the middle.

If you are interested, there are gazillions of books and courses that will teach you the basics or give you the space to practice meditation. Find a technique that suits you and practise it on a regular basis.

➤ *Get organised.* Be clear about what you need to achieve today. Have your list of tasks in a prominent place where you can tick them off once they are done. Some people list items on a whiteboard. Others use web apps such as www.teuxdeux.com or www.rememberthemilk .com. I am a fan of writing tasks in my paper diary and then highlighting the ones I have completed.

Make technology work for you

We live in the communication age. Because of mobile phones and the internet we tend to be available much of the time. These distractions can interrupt our productivity hundreds of times a day. Luckily, there is as much technology designed to help your productivity as there is to hinder it. Try some of these techniques to make technology work for you:

➤ *Change to flight mode.* Unless you need the internet for your work, switch your laptop and mobile phone to flight mode when working so that you don't get notifications, emails or calls.

➤ *Break your day down into a list of 20- or 30-minute goals.* Set a timer and work through them one at a time with a little break and a pat on the back each time you tick something off the list.

☞ *Create alerts on your phone for each part of a planned day.* If you find you are doing something other than what you'd planned, the next alert will remind you to get focused.

☞ *Use background noise generators.* Your productivity and focus can be aided significantly by listening to ambient music or white noise as you work. There are many websites — such as www.coffitivity.com, www.ambient-mixer.com and www.noisli.com — that will give you free background noise in a variety of settings, such as café sounds and nature sounds. Many websites also have mobile apps that give you similar options offline. I use background noise generators whenever I want to get serious with my work!

Form productive habits

Being productive is a habit that you can develop. You can train your brain to be ready to work and be focused. One of the key elements of this is to create a routine for productivity. Here are some ways you can do that:

☞ *Get up an hour earlier than usual.* Ignore how tired you feel, go directly to your work station and begin working.

☞ *Create a physical routine prior to working.* A routine such as a 20-minute brisk walk will give you something that you can emulate every time you want your brain to know it is time to work.

☞ *Start with the hard tasks.* When planning your actions, choose something hard to start with and celebrate its completion! You are much better off to do the hard things when you are fresh, and it is motivating to have those tasks behind you.

☞ *Set short time frames.* If you tend to leave things to the last minute, create really short time frames. Why wait six months to cram it all in? You can cram it all in now and be closer to your goal.

🖙 *Reset yourself.* If you find yourself procrastinating, take yourself physically away from your workspace, 'reset' and then come back and get into it. Your reset could be making a cup of tea, doing 20 press-ups, playing with the dog or taking a 20-minute walk.

Build a support system

Having the right people around you can make all the difference when it comes to productivity. When we are young we have teachers and parents pushing us; as adults we have our bosses. When you create your own project it is important to find people who will challenge and hold you to account too:

🖙 *Find a 'boss'.* If you find you don't work as hard for yourself as you do for an employer, look at what it is that you find so motivating about your boss and emulate it in your own work. You can probably find what you need from a coach or mentor — someone you report to on a regular basis with your progress and who will work with you over the long run.

🖙 *Find a partner to share the journey with.* You may have the same goals or be working on completely different projects. Either way, find someone you can meet with at least weekly or call daily to work through what you have achieved and what you plan to achieve.

🖙 *Create a community of people who understand your goals and will cheer you from the sidelines.* This can be as simple as announcing your goals and progress on Facebook, your blog or to a community you are already a part of.

If procrastination is a challenge you face regularly, work through these ideas until you find something that works for you. I find that different things impact me in different ways. Sometimes additional exercise means I can maintain my focus. For some parts of the year I am very motivated by my diary or to-do lists, but not at other times! At the time of writing, I find that ambient noise generators are the most effective way to get started and maintain my focus.

Chapter 7

Get moving

I am writing this chapter from a luxury cruise ship in the Galapagos Islands. I am sitting in the dining room looking out as we pass a beautiful, rocky outcrop where thousands of exotic birds mate, penguins and turtles swim and sea lions lounge on the white sand beaches.

We have just spent the morning snorkelling and exploring, and after a hot shower I have some free time before a delicious lunch is served. I am sipping herbal tea and eating chocolates, and loving the fact that this is my life, and because we review tours and cruises, this is my work!

Rewind to four years ago when I was sitting in the kitchen-office of my shared house, working seven days a week on my projects. I had huge debts and struggled to pay my rent — let alone the bills. The idea of a social life was so far from reality that I slowly trained my friends not to call me for events, parties and fun. I was always working.

I bought festival tickets and concert tickets and then sold them the week before I should have gone because I couldn't afford to go.

I worked and worked and didn't seem to be achieving anything. I was going in circles with project after project, passionate about many things but with no clear direction. I was feeling lost at sea.

How did I get from one extreme to the other?

What is the secret?

First, there is no secret. There is an old saying that goes, 'your luck in life is made up of 80 per cent hard work, 10 per cent luck and 10 per cent talent'.

After the experiences of the past 10 years of my life, I would say that this is absolutely true.

But to go from nothing to something, you need to get the ball rolling.

The seeds of momentum

Think of an idea or a goal as the seed of an apple tree. The seed is small, yet the promise of what it could become is much bigger.

But that something bigger is only possible if you take the seed, discover what conditions apple trees need for growing, plant the seed in a good spot, water it, ensure it has the right nutrients, and protect it from disease and being trampled on or eaten when it is small.

Once it reaches a certain stage the tree will be big enough that it is no longer as vulnerable as before. At another point, it will bear fruit and all of your efforts will pay off when you can pick it and sell it or make it into apple crumble.

At this stage, you could even consider planting an orchard to expand the results of your efforts. But even if you get busy and ignore your first tree, it may propagate itself over time and new trees will spring up around it without your help and input.

This is called *momentum*.

The process of creating momentum starts when you plant the first seeds; and this is what we focus on now to get one of your dreams on the path to reality, just as Randall did in this story.

 Case study: making a life out of making a difference

By the time Randall Howlett had finished his degree in landscape surveying he was already certain it was not the job for him.

He worked in his profession for several years, but when a new boss decided he didn't like him from the outset, Randall looked to pursue something he had developed a passion for: tourism.

While travelling in London he got his first gig by chance, taking a tour group for a week in Pamplona, Spain. Although he loved every moment, he still found himself going back to the familiarity of work as a surveyor.

One day he had had enough. Randall quit his job and bought a one-way ticket to Darwin. He soon found a job as a tour guide in Alice Springs and fell in love with the work. He loved that it was part of his job to learn about the history, the fauna and the flora. He was a natural guide and it was a job he thrived in.

He saved up and bought a round-the-world ticket, but in Guatemala his travel plans changed when he found a not-for-profit trekking organisation called Quetzal Trekkers. The organisation funded local children's charities, and within a month he was the head guide. Five years later he had found a balance that had him guiding in the European summers to earn a living and then volunteer guiding in Guatemala the rest of the year to raise money for the community. He started to see the not-for-profit model as a real way to benefit developing communities.

(continued)

Case study: making a life out of making a difference *(cont'd)*

One day, Randall heard about some great grassroots organisations in Sucre, Bolivia, that really needed funding. He went to visit, fell in love with the area and saw an opportunity to explore a dream of opening a not-for-profit trekking company and café.

A few months later he arrived with $7000 and started a trekking organisation. Three years later he added a restaurant. Condor Trekkers and Condor Café now fund school supplies around Sucre, a library, water pumps and composting toilets in remote communities, daily nutritious meals for disadvantaged kindergarten children and much more. It employs and empowers more than 20 staff who are thrilled to not only have a chance to improve their own lives, but also to take an active role in the community. Today Randall is ready to leave the organisation to the locals he has trained so that he can start up again in another community somewhere in the world. See **www.condortrekkers.org**

Building momentum

When starting new projects many people expect to see results immediately and if they don't, they give up. The problem with this is that you never know how long it will take for your project to gain momentum until momentum actually starts occurring.

Once you are doing everything you know has to be done, there is usually a point where things start to get exciting and where your project starts to take on a life of its own. Depending on the size and longevity of your project, this can happen many times, but the first time, especially if you have been working on it for some time, is often the sweetest.

When we decided that we would visit inspiring people in Latin America and film their stories, there were a lot of unknowns for us — in fact, all of it was unknown!

We knew what we wanted to achieve but only had a few of the skills, contacts and resources we needed to make it a reality.

We were starting a new project from scratch, so there was no momentum. We knew our project's success would depend entirely on our passion and hard work to begin with, and along the way, if we kept up the intensity, we would start to build momentum.

Sometimes, though, a lot comes down to luck. I talk about luck a lot. I am lucky to have been born with health and parents who loved me. I am lucky to have had the experiences I had as a child and the opportunity to travel. I am lucky for the bad experiences as well as the good, as I learned many lessons and lived to tell the tale. I am lucky that I have not been hit by a bus or fallen in a pothole! I am lucky that I have a reasonable degree of intelligence and can articulate myself in a way that I am understood by most of the people I communicate with.

To add to that, I truly believe the harder you work, the luckier you get.

The harder you work, the more opportunities present themselves, and the more willing you are to make the most of them.

The harder you work, the more you put yourself out there and the more momentum you build.

The harder you work, the more likely you are to reach your goals.

Hard work does not guarantee you anything, but it certainly gives you more chances of success.

But what if you are inherently lazy?

Procrastination, laziness and avoidance all give you similar results: a lack of power to achieve the things you want to achieve in life.

For some people this is such a strong habit that you avoid even having goals in the first place. You may dumb down the urge with alcohol, drugs or anger, or just pretend that you don't care. But this can be hard work too!

It is hard work to spend your whole life pretending not to care and pretending that you are not suffering by living an unsatisfying life.

Would you prefer to work hard on exciting goals that have the potential to bring you great satisfaction and a fulfilling lifestyle, or would you prefer to work hard suffering through your unfulfilled existence?

It's your choice.

I believe humans have an inherent need to contribute, relate, learn and achieve. When you are not contributing, relating, learning and achieving, you leave the door open for dissatisfaction and depression. Creating a lifestyle where you are needed, useful and appreciated in the world is a powerful experience that will help ensure a fulfilling life.

What do you really need to know?

It is normal not to know what you are doing when you embark on a new project or set a new goal. That feeling will disappear as you get more experience and gain more knowledge. It is amazing how much you can learn in six months or one year, so the sooner you start, the better — regardless of how ready you feel you are.

When working towards any new goal, I write a list of all the things I will need to know in order to be successful and, against that, what I already know and have experience in. Invariably, you find out more about your needs along the way, but it helps to start somewhere.

Five Point Five: our need-to-know list

Things we already have experience with:

- how to produce a blog/website

- how to write blogs

- how to use social media for marketing the website.

Things to learn/discover:

- how to film and edit mini-documentaries

- how to take and edit photos for our website

- how to approach sponsors and partners

- how to find representatives of community projects who are willing to be filmed

- how to make our travel lifestyle sustainable

- how to speak Spanish.

When we first wrote this list we didn't even have the technical equipment we needed to do the filming. We had a lot to learn. We spoke to dozens of people about what we needed and how best to go about it.

In the end we realised that we didn't know anyone specifically with experience filming mini-documentaries, so we also did a lot of research, watched a lot of videos and read a lot of e-books.

We were looking for a production team to help us edit the videos, but didn't find what we were looking for. Meanwhile, John started playing with video-editing software and then found he not only enjoyed it but had a talent for storytelling. Only later did we realise how crucial that would be to the project's success.

(continued)

Five Point Five: our need-to-know list *(cont'd)*

We knew we needed to approach sponsors but had no idea how it all worked, what they would need or how to make our offer competitive against the other funding requests they were likely to receive.

We took a good look at our concept to decide what kind of companies we would like to work with and what kind of companies would potentially want to work with us.

From there we worked with a friend who has experience drafting grant proposals and similar types of documents and she helped us shape a letter to potential sponsors.

In the meantime we looked at the types of sponsors we wanted to work with. Most of their websites had information on the types of projects they were interested in and the process we needed to go through to apply for funding.

In addition, I called many people in my phone book to see if they knew people who could help us. We made some good connections that way and were given plenty more helpful and useful information.

Next we needed to find community projects in Latin America that were willing to be filmed. Again, I had no idea where to start! How would we find them? How would we speak to them when we couldn't speak Spanish? Would they even be interested in working with us? How invasive would they consider filming to be? Is it even appropriate? Could we do a good job of telling their story? How else could we support them with our videos?

One day I attended a blogging conference and, over drinks, I started talking to a woman from World Vision Australia. It was really exciting to meet her and get her opinion about our idea from the perspective of a major charity.

She loved it! In fact, at that time they were creating a blog ambassador program that we could be a part of. This was a great boost to our confidence—not only would charities potentially be interested in working with us, but they may be able to help us in some ways too.

As well as the reality of this new project, we had to work out how to make a long-term travelling lifestyle sustainable! The longest I had ever been travelling as an adult was 12 weeks; the longest John and I had travelled together as a couple was four weeks.

We had many questions to answer: What will our relationship be like if we travel together for three years? What will it be like to work together on a big project like this? Will my income streams hold up and cover costs long term? Could John also create mobile income streams? How will we keep our costs down while we start this expensive new project?

We decided that all we could do was take all the actions we knew to take and see what happened!

This may sound blasé, but if you think about life as a series of uncertainties (which it is) and accept that there are no guarantees about anything (because there aren't), then you can work on the assumption that all you can do in life is the best thing you know to do right now. Sometimes it will work out beautifully and sometimes it will fail, in which case you learn the lesson and start again.

In terms of learning Spanish, we ran out of time before we left. Instead we immersed ourselves in the language when we arrived in Latin America and started learning out of sheer necessity.

Once we began working out what we needed to know and started to take the actions to get what we needed, there was a huge bunch of practicalities that made the project still feel illusive. For example:

➪ What would we need to take?

➪ How much would everything cost?

➪ How would we carry or transport all the stuff we needed?

➪ Who might be interested in joining our team and how would we find them?

➪ How would we manage the whole project?

➪ How would we stay connected to keep my business running?

➪ What is the best way to film a mini-documentary?

➪ Would we need a whole new website or could we incorporate Five Point Five into something we already had?

The list went on and on and on!

We kept a running list of these practicalities and addressed each of them in turn by asking around and finding people who were nearly always very willing to help us with the answers.

Action: list what you need to learn and the practical issues to address

Write a list of things you will need to learn and discover along the way. Also, consider the practical issues you will need to work through in order to get your project off the ground and keep it moving forward. Add to these lists and mark things 'complete' as you go. Let's use the sailing example again.

We need to learn and gain experience in:
- how to manage the practical maintenance of the boat in all sorts of situations
- CPR, first aid, water rescue, and so on
- how to fish and prepare fresh fish.

Practical issues:
- What do we need to take with us? What can we find along the way?
- What should we consider for travel insurance?
- What licensing regulations do we need to comply with (if any)?
- How will we fundraise and create compelling sponsorship proposals?
- Can the kids skip a year of school and not be penalised by the system?

Knowledge is a distraction

Have you noticed that we have an obsession with information? We are looking for more, more, more — often we will forgo what we are supposed to be doing or are paid to be doing, in order to read more, consume more and learn more.

The problem is that only so much knowledge will help you fulfil your dreams; everything else is a distraction. However, we often use our lack of knowledge or experience as a (seemingly) valid excuse for not taking action.

I often speak to people who are putting off getting started because they need to get one more degree or qualification. Unless your dream is to be a surgeon or something requiring a specialty skill or specific experience, there is usually a way to get started right now, *in some way*. If more knowledge is really essential to your dream being fulfilled, consider how you can create momentum *while* you do the necessary training or learning.

The problem with knowledge in general is that it does not make a huge difference to your chances of success. Take fitness, for example. Most unfit people *know how* to get fit, but knowing makes no difference! It is not until you put on your runners and get out there every day that you will actually experience what it feels like to be fit and healthy. Only then will you start to see a change in your muscle tone.

It is the reason university graduates often do internships and work for free. Their education will help them understand important concepts and get their foot in the door, but the real learning is the experience of working in the real world, with real situations.

I experienced this firsthand when I arrived in Australia. I was 21 and my new employer hired me because I had the specific experience he was looking for. All of my new colleagues were in their thirties and forties, well educated, mostly male and not at all impressed with this young high-school dropout in their midst.

At 21, most people my age were finishing university and looking for jobs. I, however, had six years of work experience and career progression and found myself playing with the big kids.

In the game of life, you will only create momentum and give yourself a chance of fulfilling your dreams by *taking action*. Regardless of how much knowledge you have you still have to take the first step ... and then the second step.

As a coach, I have spoken to hundreds of people about getting started. Not one of them *had* to wait to get started on their dream project, regardless of their level of knowledge. This applies even for the complete newbies.

People are often shocked by how simple it would be for them to get started on the parts they *can* start now. You don't have to change the world overnight. Getting started, in most cases, is as simple as choosing a name for your project or making some phone calls.

People often look at a big goal and then get stopped by the enormity of it all. But everything can and must be done in small steps. Don't get overwhelmed by what you want to accomplish — just consider what you can accomplish today. If you are time-poor, get up 30 minutes earlier every day and get started. In a world of busy people with limited resources, some will rise to the top and succeed at the things they dream of. There is no reason why it shouldn't be you.

Discover and create opportunities

When striving for the seemingly impossible, you need to pull at the resources available to you and look for new opportunities. Opportunities come in many shapes and forms and there are usually as many opportunities as you have thoughts in your head. If you lack opportunities, you are probably not being creative or bold enough to look for them.

The more you look, the more opportunities you will see and be able to take advantage of. There will literally be thousands. Being creative about recognising the opportunities you have will give you plenty to choose from, and when you have plenty to choose from you can keep taking action and keep building your momentum.

There are opportunities out there to help overcome every challenge you face. If you can't see them, start having conversations with other people, as it's often the case that other people can see what you can't. Don't stop talking and asking until you can see a way out of the difficulty or challenge you face.

When looking for opportunities it pays to go wild — consider *every* opportunity, however outrageous. If you don't have the money to achieve your goal, for example, look at how you can raise the money, or look at how you can do it with no money. If you don't have the expertise to achieve your goal, look at who does and consider what you could exchange for their expertise.

Five Point Five: how we created opportunities

Although I had created a flexible income with my business, it was still in its infancy and not rich enough to provide for both of us as well as a resource-hungry new project.

We looked at mobile income opportunities for John and at the same time started to consider ways we could offset our costs. One of the large costs when travelling is accommodation, and because we wanted to write, make films, have access to a nice kitchen and enjoy some peace and quiet as a married couple, it was important to us that we stayed in comfortable and private spaces away from the daily party that is associated with many backpackers' adventures.

We started to brainstorm possible ways to offset our accommodation costs.

After considering a dozen possible opportunities, the two that really appealed were house-and-pet-sitting and exchanging services for accommodation.

We started to research both and found that although house-and-pet-sitting would be perfect for us, there was not a huge range of options in Latin America. So we put the idea on hold until we were destined for continents that had more opportunities.

Meanwhile we realised that with John's burgeoning skills in filming and editing videos and my experience with social media and marketing, we had something that could be of great value to hotels and travel companies.

We started to talk to the hotel owners we would meet along the way about what they needed help with and it was quickly apparent that many needed more help with marketing. We came up with a plan and sent it out to a few hotels in Colombia. The response was great, so we booked in our first jobs. We would stay in their hotel for up to a week and create a video review that would help potential guests see the place in more detail.

Meanwhile the hotels would get a beautiful quality video they could use in all their marketing.

For us, this arrangement worked for so many reasons, such as:

- we got to connect with like-minded business owners in each location, and work together for mutual benefit

- we could stay in the best and most beautiful places at no cost

- the money we saved on accommodation costs could be diverted into growing our project.

The hotel owners would often be able to help us find small grassroots community projects that we may have otherwise missed.

We definitely don't expect to get something for nothing. John works very hard on the videos, but it is a created opportunity that works perfectly to let us live the lifestyle we like to live.

We have now branched out into tours and cruises and have wonderful luxury experiences as a result. We have also struck up many warm friendships and business partnerships.

Hearing *no* will not break the skin

My philosophy about creating opportunities is: 'Don't be afraid to ask for what you want'. The worst thing people can say is *no*.

Opportunities are there for the making and taking. The only thing stopping you is the bounds of your imagination and the confidence to ask for what you need to succeed.

If you are going to create a life-changing project, it is likely you will need or benefit from outside help along the way. Being able to ask for what you want and need is something that will be enormously beneficial. As humans we tend to avoid asking things of people if we fear they may say *no*. For many people *no* is the worst thing they can hear—in fact, some people experience the word *no* as a total rejection. Some people experience a *no* as if they have been physically attacked.

As a result, we often find ourselves reluctant to say *no* and we are terrified of hearing *no* to our requests. Living this way will not help you or your project!

If your project requires sponsors, partners, funding, fundraising, mentors, supporters, fans or any form of outside assistance, there will be times when you need to be able to make requests.

To get what you want, you must ask for what you need until someone says *yes*. Even though it may seem terrifying, there is no risk in asking. As I said before, the worst they can say is *no*! However much it sucks, hearing *no* will not pierce your skin or give you a nosebleed. It will not make you collapse or put you in the hospital.

In my experience, there are only a finite number of *no*s until you get a *yes*. It could be one, dozens or even hundreds, but you will get there if you persist.

The new kid on the block

If you are new to the scene that will be the focus of your project, it helps to immerse yourself in it and surround yourself with people involved in it. You are far more likely to find exciting opportunities if you are talking about your project with people who already have an interest in what you are doing.

There are plenty of ways to get involved. Online you could write a blog, join relevant forums and be part of the conversations related to what you're doing. You can also start conversations with like-minded people on Twitter or with members of relevant Facebook groups.

In person you can do courses, have coffee with people of interest and attend relevant events and gatherings.

The more you are involved, talk and mingle, the more comfortable you will be in your new community and the more opportunities will present themselves to you.

If you are new, it also helps if you are generous with your time and know-how. The more you can contribute to your new community, the quicker you will build relationships and become an essential part of the crew.

Stretch your limits

The life you are living right now is a function of how big or small you have dared to dream so far. Your highs will be dizzying — or not — depending on what you consider to be possible and doable. Your lows very much depend on the strength of your fears and expectations.

External influences impact us all, and often, and we can do little to control them. What we can impact is how we react, our mindset, our actions and our belief in our own potential.

To achieve goals that are bigger than you previously thought possible, you must behave differently and do more than you previously thought possible. This stretch may be painful or joyful; it may be exciting or terrifying. Your experience of it will depend entirely on your attitude towards going beyond the point where you would normally give up.

To expand the realm of what is possible, you must expand your expectations and the amount of energy you are willing to put in. This will create bursts of new opportunity, excitement and results, which, over time, will change the way you look at the world.

If you are reading this book you are probably interested in expanding your life in some way. This is a good start for stretching your limitations! As well as taking on a life-changing project, here are some other ways you can stretch your limits.

Do things you wouldn't normally do

Are there things you 'don't do'? We generally don't do certain things because we are afraid of them in some way. I have met people who won't try new foods, dance, travel or drive on motorways. I have met people who, at 25, say they would never get married or have kids. I have met people who want to write but would never blog, and people who would rather eat their own arm (so to speak) than learn how to meditate. Basically there are many things that most of us have eliminated as possibilities or opportunities because, even without having experienced them, we have decided they are not our thing.

I had a fear of public speaking, both to audiences and to a camera. This has plagued me my entire life. At first I just *accepted* that speaking was for other people. More recently I have challenged and challenged and challenged myself to get some confidence in speaking publicly.

After the positive experience I had with the 'How to Retire in 12 Months' challenge I decided to take it more seriously. I booked in with a neuro-linguistic programming (NLP) coach and together we set a huge challenge to make me into a public speaker. Meanwhile, my husband (John) and I already had plans to leave Australia, and when we left I suddenly became the presenter in our mini-documentaries and travel reviews.

This was the most awkward part of our new project because I am not a natural-born presenter. In the beginning I was nervous, self-conscious and extremely uncomfortable in front of the camera. The situation was further exacerbated by the fact that it is actually very tough to find picturesque places in foreign cities with no background noise and good light. We would sometimes spend hours walking around or in taxis looking for a suitable spot. Then, after setting up the camera and all the sound gear we would film take after take after take just to get a single minute of introduction for our little films.

On many occasions curious people would come to watch, which just made me more self-conscious, or it would start to rain, or car alarms would go off nearby. All of this stalled the process and made me more anxious. If there was a lot of drama, John would start to get frustrated, and I would get even more flustered because he was frustrated. Then every week or two we would do it all again!

At one point I presented an introduction to a hotel and we got it on the second take. Two weeks later I presented three introductions. I was sick, but I managed to churn them out like a trooper. Something had changed — I now had experience doing these little introductions on camera and it was beginning to show. It was easier and I was more flexible. I could even be a little creative in the process. I also discovered that it was infinitely better if we were organised about what I needed to say.

Nowadays, if you asked me to talk to a crowded room, or if I was in front of a film crew with giant cameras, I may not be as confident as I am with my own video projects. However, now that I have presented more than 30 stories, I can feel it in my bones that I am a presenter with a year and a half of experience in front of the camera. It may never be something I am truly comfortable with, but I did not let it limit the opportunities available to me and, ironically, presenting is now an important part of my amazing new life!

Look at the things that you refuse to do or are afraid of doing. Make a list of them. Set a date, make whatever arrangements you need to make and then do them! Overcoming the main things that stop you will completely stretch your limits and open many doors that you never thought possible. I recently printed business cards and on them I added 'Presenter' to my previous titles of 'Business Coach', 'Writer', and 'Blogger'. This innocuous little word on my card was a victory over a lifelong fear.

Learn something you've always wanted to learn

Another way to stretch your limits is to immerse yourself in a brand-new skill. Learning something exciting will add spice to your life and remind you that you are never too old to learn something new. In my twenties I started to mourn the things I had not learned when I was a child: another language, the guitar, how to knit, graphic design and my multiplication tables, to name just a few!

In my thirties I stopped mourning and starting learning: learning a new language, learning new skills and being crafty again. Some things have been a lot of work to learn! I have been slowly learning Spanish for one and a half years and I find it hard. Harder still because I was absent from school when they taught much of the structure of the English language!

What I am finding is that after a few years of learning exciting new things, I feel like I am learning faster now. It feels like my brain needed to remember what it was to be a child when everything was new and seemingly much easier to learn.

To stretch your limits, choose one thing that you have been aching to be good at. It doesn't matter what it is, but it has to be something that is exciting to you. Find a teacher, buy the books, tools or instruments you need and/or register for a course that will give you the basics.

Twelve months from now you will have an exciting hobby that could even lead to a fulfilling career, business or new way of life. In addition, it will boost your confidence that you can learn new things, all of which will help you move towards achieving your dream life goals.

Practical steps for success

Here are seven practical steps to get you and your project moving on the path to success.

1 Contact people who could help you

The more people you speak to, make requests of, connect with and inspire with your project, the more opportunities will come your way. Remember, for every call you make, the worst they can say is *no*. On the flipside, every person you speak to has the potential to open the door to opportunities that could either take it to new levels, in exciting new directions, or help you solve some of the challenges you are facing at any given moment.

2 Prioritise

It's time to get straight about your life: there are things that are crucial to health, happiness and fulfilment, and there are plenty of things that we obsess over and waste time doing that are not crucial to our success.

Yes, it is nice to have a clean house and all the washing done and to have a lovely shine on the car. But will you think about that on your death bed? Is it really worth stressing over and choosing instead of your dreams? If you were achieving the goals on your bucket list, what would become less important?

In my experience, a huge number of the things that were important to me are no longer important now that I am living a life that I designed. The reality is that if you need to find an extra two hours a day to make your dreams come true, you have to give up two hours of what you may have been doing otherwise. That may be time that you would otherwise spend shopping, cleaning the house, socialising, reading, watching television, surfing the internet, or talking on the phone.

Do what you need to do to make the time to pursue your life-changing projects. Change your habits, prioritise what you must do and then figure out solutions for the rest.

We have as many options as we can think of, so if you are feeling trapped with your responsibilities, get creative! Brainstorm 20 ways you could approach a situation. Go wild with possible alternatives. Some may end up being too fanciful or silly, but at least you are seeing the options. And you never know, some of the most outrageous alternatives may actually be possible, so don't limit yourself to doing things the way you have always done them.

3 Get other people involved

Build a team of people to lead and/or participate in growing your project and achieving its goals. Somewhere along the way we, in this modern, so-called civilised First World, gave up our place in communities and became millions of individuals surviving our lives by ourselves in our own little worlds. This is not conducive to success.

Building a community of people involved in your project makes it a lot easier to realise your goal and it's so much more fun to celebrate the win with them all.

For the majority of people this is not easy. You need to rely on people, be a leader and be open to suggestion and contribution. In turn, you need to be reliable, allow others to lead and be keen and willing to contribute in new ways. None of these things are taught in mainstream schools, but they are so critical to our success in life.

Interpersonal relationships are often fraught with miscommunications, misunderstandings and a lack of empathy. You may be working with the loveliest people in the world, but each person comes with their perspective, experience and judgements. When the relationship works, your project can happen like sunshine and lollipops; when it doesn't, it can drag your project down into the depths of failure and despair.

Finding the right people for your project and understanding how to work well with them is something you will need to learn along the way. An added difficulty here is that because we are seldom trained for this, you will probably screw up from time to time! Long term, however, mastering the skills associated with team building and teamwork could be the difference between success and failure. These skills will enable your project to grow and positively impact your whole family or dozens, hundreds or thousands of lives, as well as your own. Now wouldn't that be awesome!

4 Jump out of bed in the morning

Are you someone who drags yourself out of bed in the morning? Do you press 'snooze' five times before you get up? For many years, getting up was the most painful part of my day. Several years ago someone told me that they tried a new way to start the day. As soon as they became conscious in the morning, their first thought was to jump out of bed and shout, 'Bring it on!' I thought this was just crazy enough that it could work. I decided that instead of suffering for 30 minutes in the morning before I got up and then suffering until I had a coffee, I would jump out of bed excited about the day. I would consciously choose to enjoy waking up.

Now, this didn't quite happen every day, but over the course of the next few months I became a morning person. I trained myself to have energy in the morning and to be excited about getting up. This is something that has completely altered my life! Now when I wake up, my brain switches on with excitement in the mornings and if I get something done first thing, I have a sense of achievement all day that inspires me to be more productive.

Do I do this all the time? *No!* But I realise now that I can control how well my days go. I am no longer a victim of mornings. Years after discovering this I live with completely different expectations of myself. It is also a powerful reminder of just how important it is that you give yourself the right messages and are responsible for each part of your existence — even the bits that you feel victim to.

5 Do things you wouldn't normally do

Your comfort zone is like the dead zone of what is possible in your life. If you continue to strive for what you already know is possible, you are training your brain to stop developing. To make the impossible, possible, you must habitually challenge your idea of what is possible. If you are constantly challenging yourself, you will allow your dreams to get bigger and bigger and this is what will give you the possibility of life-changing and thrilling adventures.

So learn new things, and put yourself in new and uncomfortable situations every day. Challenge yourself to overcome your fears and put your brain to work. The more you do this, the more excitement and passion you will have for life. Do courses, read books, meet new people, learn new skills and languages, volunteer, help people, encourage the people around you and say *yes* to things you would normally say *no* to. The options are endless for what you can do that will challenge you and help you grow.

6 Say *yes!*

As young kids we are like sponges, open to suggestion, excitement and opportunity. As we grow we are exposed to thousands of experiences, including times when we may have failed or been hurt, or felt embarrassed or disappointed. When something bad happens, we tend to make decisions to help avoid, or defend ourselves against, that kind of result again.

The problem with this 'safe' way of living is that it also closes the door to the opportunities you need in order to live the life you want to live. You cut out the bad, but you also cut out the good.

These automatic responses to new things and situations may be the very thing that is stopping you from having the success and life you dream of.

There are lots of things you can do to alter your mindset, but one sure-fire way to shake up your life is to start saying *yes* — all of the time. Say *yes* to things that you are afraid of or that you have no time for. Say *yes* to things you would normally avoid or have never done. Say *yes* to things that may surprise the people who are asking you.

Also start to notice the times when you cut potential opportunities short because you have already decided how they will turn out based on your previous experiences. If you are looking for an exciting new future that is completely different from your past, you need to see it that way! Your past experiences and memories are no use to you in your exciting new existence and the only way to change is by altering how you behave right now.

Note: for people who always say *yes*, the opposite may apply here! In this case, say *no* to things you would normally say *yes* to. Shake up the world as you know it.

7 Always look for new ways to achieve the impossible

Making the impossible, possible, is something you can get experience in. The more impossible things you make possible, the better you will become at it, and the more you will believe in yourself. Children do this over and over as they learn how to speak, walk, ride bikes and do cartwheels.

My priority is to spend much of my time on my laptop, creating, connecting and writing. I am motivated to get fit from time to time, but have never sustained a good level of fitness. But this doesn't stop me from taking on big physical challenges occasionally that completely knock me out! My belief in my ability is much stronger than my physical strength and so I am the person who arrives first at the

12-hour volcano climb and then hobbles out last and can't walk for a week.

During my first trapeze lesson, excitement and adrenalin meant I had more swings than the rest of the group, but my upper body was crippled until just before I took my second lesson.

When we were planning to travel for three years our estimated expenses were much greater than our earnings. As such, it didn't seem possible that we could sustain the expense of the new project, our lifestyle and everything else for two people. Yet two years later we are still here and going strong.

Developing a habit of achieving the impossible will set you up for the big projects you are interested in. The more impossible things you attempt to achieve, the more likely you are to succeed in the long run. You may not have experience in the project or the challenge itself, but you will have experience in facing challenges in general. Get as much experience as possible in achieving goals you deem impossible and you will find that many thrilling opportunities arrive on your doorstep.

Chapter 8

Commitment, confidence and courage

It's not news that your attitude to life is what creates your life. Likewise, your attitude will affect every part of your project and your ability to succeed in reaching your goals. So if you want dramatically different results, it is time to change it up: you need to develop a completely different attitude and belief in yourself.

The truth about commitment

What does your commitment look like? We all have the ability to commit or not to commit in any situation. There will be some things in your life that you completely commit to, but think about how often we do things without being committed to them. We just go through the motions. We do it because we feel we have to, rather than because we *really want* to. This usually produces unexciting results. Commitment can be a major determining factor in whether we succeed or fail.

If you are 100 per cent committed to your job, for example, you may bounce out of bed in the morning, get in early, take leadership roles when the opportunity arises, talk about it excitedly with your friends and family, and gladly take on extra responsibilities when you can see new opportunities or areas for improvement and growth.

There will be some areas of your life where you display a 100 per cent commitment without realising that you are doing so. It may be to things that give you some sort of pleasure, such as playing video games, cooking lush meals or going to the gym, watching television or posting to Instagram, Facebook or Twitter.

There will also be some areas where you do not display commitment, even though you technically are committed in some way. You may be physically there, but have your attention elsewhere. You complete the task, but it is a poor representation of what you could have created if you had cared more. A job or a person you fell out of love with are two obvious examples of this.

Think about all the things you are committed to in your life — everything you spend your time, money and/or energy on, in all areas of your life.

Now think about each thing from an outsider's perspective. If a commitment inspector were to follow you around for a month, what would they say you are committed to? What would they say you are not really committed to?

What would they say you give the most time, money and energy to? Where would they see you just going through the motions?

Would you be proud or embarrassed of their findings?

Going through the motions

When creating a life-changing project, some people find a whole new level of energy and they will work night and day until they get what they want. Their level of commitment is clear and they will blow themselves and everyone else away with their passion and how much they can achieve.

Most people's commitment levels, however, tend to waver. They may start out strong and excited but then the commitment wears off after a few weeks. They may pick it up again after an exciting conversation or event, but it falls apart a few days later for some other reason. There are actually many reasons why your commitment levels may waver, including:

➩ a fear (of failure or success)

➩ experiencing failure, disappointment or setbacks

➩ a lack of confidence

➩ becoming overwhelmed

➩ caring too much about what other people think.

Lack of commitment can be a sneaky beast. We start a new job, project or relationship eager and motivated and then something happens. We lose the motivation we once had and wither, get bored, take it for granted or start to feel unsatisfied. If that happens, we either give up or fall into autopilot and start to go through the motions.

Going through the motions is nasty, because from the outside people may not realise how uncommitted you have become. You can fool yourself and everybody else that you are giving it your all when really you are just being there.

Going through the motions is terribly dissatisfying. Yet many of us do it, in many areas of our lives. At the same time many of us run defensive arguments through our minds in case we get caught out! This can be exhausting and stressful, and it is a complete waste of time and energy.

Losing your commitment to your project will undoubtedly give you poor results and will likely lead to the demise of your dreams. The good thing is that you have the power to alter this state of mind. You have the power to completely change your situation just by giving yourself the space to recommit.

Being able to recognise a lack of commitment and choosing to recommit is a powerful way of getting your project back on track.

Learning to be accountable to yourself

Many people behave one way when working for a boss, leader or company, and behave completely differently when working for themselves. This is one of the biggest problems people face when starting their first business or creating a life-changing project.

If you have no external person or group of people holding you to account, then who will? Finding your personal drive will not only help you reach your goals, it will give you a new level of confidence and freedom that will alter how you live your life.

When you are being accountable to yourself, you need to deal with all the issues you have with yourself. Even if you are doing the exact same work for yourself as you would be doing for someone else, you will treat it differently depending on how you view yourself in the world.

For this reason it is important to know what motivates you. Some people are motivated to work because they want to look good (or not look bad) in the eyes of their employers or colleagues. They want to shine.

Others are motivated by the sense of achievement attained by reaching targets or meeting deadlines. Others are motivated by pressure, so they may let things slide until someone or something is breathing down their neck.

To understand how you will approach your project, it is important you know what motivates you. If the factor that normally motivates you (for example, a boss) is not available as part of your project, you will need to replace the motivating factor or be aware that you could automatically let things slide unless you put prompts in place to keep you moving.

I find I am more committed when I tell people of my intention because I don't want to let people down or let them think that I am a slacker!

Knowing this, I make sure that I declare my intentions and goals to a lot of people around me. For me a blog is a great place to make these declarations to thousands of people. So is publishing my bucket list in this book!

Basically, you need to understand how to motivate yourself to take action on your project as if your life depended on it (which it does).

Three steps for inspiring recommitment

If you find you have lost commitment to your project (or anything else for that matter) here is a simple three-step process that will help you regain your passion and recommit to achieving your goal.

1 Analyse how you operate

Because of the way our brains work, we are creatures of habit who naturally think and act in distinguishable patterns. When it comes to commitment, you will have patterns of behaviour that you will be able to track back throughout your adult life. For example, many people find they have similar problems in different relationships. Many people find they attract the same kinds of people over and over. You will find that you generally have some similar pains and successes in each of your jobs, projects, relationships and friendships. Without realising it, you have *designed* your life this way because it is familiar.

For some people confrontation and anger is familiar. For some people feeling rejected or not good enough is familiar.

For some people feeling compelled to be perfect or prove something is familiar. You may not like it one bit, but it is familiar and you seek out those situations over and over in your life.

When it comes to commitment, you will also have patterns. You may be someone who gives it all until you smell failure and then you quit. You may be someone who avoids commitment completely. You may be someone who commits to something new every week. You may commit wholeheartedly to some things, but leave a back door open when it comes to other things.

Take some time to objectively analyse each part of your life and how much or little you commit to each part of it. It will be easy to spot: the parts of your life that you are most committed to are often the areas in which you are having the most success and satisfaction; the parts of your life that leave much to be desired, that are hard or that you dislike the most, are probably the areas in which you have the least commitment.

How do you behave when you are truly committed to something? How do you behave when you are very uncommitted? Where are you being uncommitted without realising it, until now?

What patterns can you see in how you end things? What patterns can you see happening before things end? Think about relationships, projects, jobs and of course other times you have set yourself big, exciting goals. What are your patterns?

At this point it helps to get an outside opinion. This can be brutal, but the truth does make a difference! Take a deep breath and ask your boss, team, friends and family where they think you could show more commitment. You may or may not enjoy the answers they give you, but either way this will help you identify your patterns.

If you know what your patterns are, you can notice them when they start to happen, and work on creating new outcomes, seeing new opportunities and experiencing results that you haven't believed possible before.

2 Create or recreate inspiring goals

When you are stuck in the everydayness of your commitment it can be easy to lose focus and see only work and responsibility. Work and responsibility for the sake of it is not a very exciting proposition. Work and responsibility that will clearly help you achieve a thrilling, life-changing goal will make the things far more rewarding on a daily basis.

If you don't have an inspiring goal, your commitment is likely to wane when things get tough, even if you keep doing the work. So, if you are finding that you have lost your commitment (or never really found it) take some time to create or recreate some tangible goals that light your fire.

Give yourself permission to dream big. What is the goal that makes all this work worthwhile? What would life be like if you made this dream a reality?

Stop for 10 minutes and visualise this goal being fulfilled. Imagine yourself there at the moment it all comes to fruition. Allow yourself to feel the joy and excitement of that moment. Create the whole situation in your mind, including the place and the people who will be there.

A few years ago I began to understand the importance of visualisation. I went to a small event and one of the exercises was to visualise the moment when a dream was realised. We wrote down the dream first, the date and the details of what the moment of realisation looked like.

A little sceptical, I wrote about a moment in time. I was flying out of Sydney airport on my way to spend six months in South America. Beside me was the man of my dreams. I indulged in the moment and saw Sydney disappearing through the little window on the plane. I allowed myself to feel the excitement that I was finally on my way. I was able to look back and see that all the work had paid off.

Later that night I put my handwritten visualisation notes on top of a pile of books beside my bed and did the visualisation exercise again. The next morning I did the exercise again and continued to do this from time to time over the next few weeks before the paper slowly slipped out of sight and I got back to the rush of normal life.

Three years later I was selling/chucking/gifting everything I owned and I found the dusty note behind a stack of books. I had since met and married the man of my dreams and was weeks away from heading to Venezuela to travel through South America.

However sceptical I may have been about visualisation, there was nothing more powerful than seeing the exact scene of my visualised goal play out in reality.

3 Make it real now

Find a way to make your future dreams part of your current activities. For example, if one of your goals is to save money for a house, then look at houses in your spare time. Read books about real estate, visit open homes and apply for a pre-approval on a loan. Be clear about what you want to buy when you have the money. Your hours spent working hard will have far more purpose if you really feel that you are in the market for your dream house.

The same principle applies to any project. Find a way to make your future goal part of your experience right now. If your goal is to sail the world with your family, stick a big poster of a boat on the kitchen wall and make a food plan for the boat. If your goal is to eliminate cruelty in factory farms, adopt a lovable rescue pet to come home to each day and remind you why you are working so hard.

Get focused once more on your goal and keep your eye firmly on the outcome, and you will find it can completely alter your commitment to your project.

Stepping forward boldly when you don't know what you're doing

You are starting or creating something completely new. What this inherently implies is that you have no experience in achieving the goals you have set for yourself.

We are continually learning, from the day we are born — that is, until we reach our twenties or thirties and slow down. Many of us become comfortable creatures of habit and 'experienced' in what we know.

This comfort zone kills opportunity because we forget how important it is to continue to learn. We are programmed to love nothing more than being 'right' and our brains revel in using our past experience and knowledge to deal with or resolve whatever new challenges confront us.

For this reason, some of us will slowly begin to reject new things because it can be uncomfortable to be the new guy (or girl) at something. We start to really believe that we are too old to learn. We dream about being good at certain things, but don't take the necessary steps to master them.

It is important that you don't allow yourself to be this way or let your lack of knowledge or experience knock your confidence in your project. To be a success your project requires you to take many actions with only your gut to guide you.

As you know, there were many things that were completely new to us when we started Five Point Five. To keep us on track we focused on being confident that we would learn what we needed to learn along the way.

Every single new project, idea, business or relationship comes with risk because it is new! Don't think that you and your project are any different from every other new project out there. The only difference is what you bring to it. You need to back your new project like only you can, because you have created it!

Confidence, attitude and action are like the womb in which your new project needs to grow to become more than an idea. You must bring a healthy amount of confidence, a positive attitude and a lot of activity to see it through to success.

Five Point Five: becoming confident

Our first mini-documentary was about two little schools run by a man in the slums of northern Colombia. We spent three weeks volunteering there to understand what he was doing and to get the footage we needed. Initially we offered to volunteer every day, but we soon realised that this wouldn't work if we intended to make the film as well.

We were new to filming, and as we hadn't volunteered much before we had to figure out how we would go working with kids. We also had to find the line between being considerate of teachers and their classes and getting the shots we needed. Another challenge was our inability to communicate with many of the people we were interviewing (as we didn't speak Spanish), so we had to rely on translators and got used to dealing with many miscommunications.

We were paranoid about all of our new gear, especially as one of the schools was in a slum many taxi drivers wouldn't drive to because they thought it was too dangerous. Bringing out cameras, microphones and other equipment in a tiny, two-room school was very disruptive and the kids would go berserk playing up for the camera, with dozens of curious hands wanting to grab and play with the new 'toys'.

We also got emotionally involved in the project and wanted to help as much as we could. We offered to interview some of the volunteers so that they could use the videos on their website.

There was an expectation and respect for our project because we were there to deliver the outcome. We said we would film a documentary. There was no time or space to doubt ourselves because we had to focus on actually doing it and learning everything as we went.

If you say you are going to create something, in other people's eyes you become what you declare yourself to be. Take Five Point Five for example: we said we would make documentaries, so as far as the charity was concerned we were documentary filmmakers. If we had dwelled on the fact that we had never made a documentary before, we would have done the charity a disservice. We would have been focusing on our own lack of experience rather than on doing the best job we could at the time.

There is a saying that 'you are only as good as your word'. When creating your life-changing project, your word is gold. If you say you are going to do something, what usually happens is that many opportunities emerge to make your word a reality. Even if you feel insecure or inexperienced, supportive people will take your word, and the goal that you have said you are working towards, at face value and believe that it is what you are going to do.

For this reason there is no place for you to dwell on your uncertainties. Your level of experience will grow as you work on your project. Your levels of confidence will increase as you start to make progress and see some successes. Giving your word on something, such as, 'We are going to make mini-documentaries' (as in our case), is a powerful declaration that you should hold in the utmost respect. To give your word and then not give your all to fulfilling it leaves you at a disadvantage because if you do this a few times you will find yourself in a community that does not believe you when you say you're going to do something; or worse, not believe in you. This will undermine your self-confidence and may close some doors on future goals you set out to achieve.

A recipe for instant confidence

Confidence. Some people seem to naturally have loads of it, and some of us need to manufacture it until we feel we have 'earned' it. When it comes to your life-changing project, confidence will give you a much better chance at success. It will enable you to:

⇨ take the actions you need to take

⇨ make decisions

⇨ make requests

⇨ explore unusual or innovative solutions

⇨ know that even if you fail, you will be okay.

Here are some confidence-building tips that will get you through any uncertain moments:

⇨ *Fake it 'til you make it.* No-one has to know you are lacking in confidence. If you are shaking violently or find yourself speechless, it may be obvious that you are nervous. However, for the most part, even if you feel really uncomfortable, only you or people who know you really well will notice!

On dozens of occasions people have told me that I didn't 'seem' nervous, when I was in fact terrified. I have come to realise that it's hard for people who don't know you very well to tell how nervous or petrified you are feeling.

Use this to your advantage. Act confident and people will treat you like you are confident. It doesn't take too many interactions for this to feel a bit more comfortable.

⇨ *Create positive affirmations.* I think personal affirmations are a bit cheesy, but I can't deny that they work! A clear and positive message repeated over and over trains your brain to think that way. Choose a positive message that you can announce regularly, out loud to the mirror, to friends or quietly in your head. Say it as many times as you can remember each day. Aim to say and think or write it at least 500 times in the morning, when you are brushing your teeth, when you are sitting on the bus or wherever you are.

Over time your brain will start to respond and remind you to think it. Eventually it will start being the soundtrack that your brain runs in the background — it becomes part of who you are.

☞ *Take a deep breath.* It is amazing how effective a deep breath can be when you are in a nerve-racking situation. Focus on your body, take long, deep breaths and quiet the intensity of your thoughts. Practise coupling this with some positive affirmations and you can learn how to generate self-confidence in moments.

☞ *Call someone for a pep talk.* Hopefully you have a coach, mentor, parent or good friend who can give you confidence in a single conversation. If not, find someone who fits the bill and set up calls with them on a regular basis, just before you head off to big meetings or before making important calls for your project. Having someone you can call on for a confidence-building pep talk can help you get through any periods of uncertainty.

☞ *Do something physical.* The endorphins you create when doing physical activity can positively impact the way you feel about yourself. If you are about to make an important call or need some confidence for a big request, find a place where you can do some push-ups or star jumps, or get off the bus early and take a brisk walk to your meeting.

When you are working on life-changing projects, sometimes you will need to do things that make you nervous. It is all part of the journey. Having a structure or person to give you confidence and support through those moments makes life a little bit easier! You are allowed to be lacking in confidence — just don't let it stop you from creating the life you dream of.

Chapter 9

Time

Lack of time and lack of money are the two most common reasons people have for not starting their life-changing projects.

If your project is large and requires a lot of money that you don't have, you could assume that you will not be able to go ahead. Likewise, if you currently have an intense job, lots of responsibilities or a young family, you may be struggling to find enough time as it is, let alone more time to start a whole new project.

Unfortunately for most people, a lack of time and money will probably be the biggest hindrances for their entire life. Fortunately it is possible for anyone to overcome these restrictions with creativity and persistence.

Because these two issues are seemingly the biggest show-stoppers for people, they each deserve their own chapter. First, let's talk about time.

The thing about time

We live in a busy world and most people who work full-time work a minimum of eight hours a day, five days a week. If you add to that time spent commuting, time spent with the kids and family, preparing food and eating, grocery shopping, walking the dog, catching up with friends, cleaning the house and doing laundry, it is understandable that you may feel you have little time to start a new hobby, let alone a life-changing project.

We are conditioned to want more and more out of life: more wealth, more responsibility, more things, bigger houses, better cars and nicer clothes.

So we get caught in a cycle of working long hours so we can keep up with the norms of a consumerist society. I believe this kind of lifestyle uses your time in a very inefficient and unsatisfying way. Unless you are doing something for a living that you love and are passionate about, living this way means you spend 40 or more hours a week to slowly increase the number and value of the things you own.

One thing you can be sure of is that your time on this planet is limited. The relationship most people have to time is recognising that it is scarce, which is true and inescapable. However long life may seem to a young person, it feels like it passes in a flash whether or not you are achieving exciting things, and that is if you are lucky enough to live very long.

For this reason it would be a real shame not to work out how you can use the time you have in the most fulfilling way possible.

Creating moments for expansion

As humans, we are remarkably adaptable. In the good times we can't imagine living any other way. But when times are tough, we make do — we adjust to the extra work, stress and responsibilities. It is not always easy to make adjustments, but we do it nonetheless. If you look back at the toughest times in your life, you will know this to be true: you survived and you probably grew stronger and more determined then than at any other time in your life.

But why should we expand in this way only when times are tough? What if you could expand now, on demand, so that you could design the life you have always dreamed of?

Expansion is often not a comfortable thing. Consider the way a muscle grows. If you use a muscle repetitively in a new way it can quickly become tired, sore and start shaking, because at this point you are tearing the muscle fibre. Over the next few days you can experience tightness and soreness as your muscle fibres heal and grow. But if you repeat the activity over a period of weeks or months your muscle will grow in strength and size and you will expand the capacity at which you can use it.

Expansion of the mind works in much the same way. Usually *something* has to happen for us to begin the process of expanding our minds to make the impossible, possible. That thing may be a huge life event such as losing someone or something we cherish, or a near miss such as an illness or accident. Or it may be more subtle, such as reading an inspiring story in the newspaper, a work change or meeting someone new. When we make a decision to expand in our mind what before has seemed impossible, we need to strengthen our mind to believe, accept and work towards the realisation of it.

What you can achieve with limited time is something you can definitely expand by strengthening your mind-muscles. I have had periods of my life where I have been busy every moment of every day, and then when challenged to take on something new I have thought it was not possible. But what I keep finding is that the act of committing to an exciting goal means I immediately get more creative and efficient with how I spend my time.

Your willingness to take on challenges that will stretch you will be the difference between having what you have and having what you want. The big question is: are you willing to do what it takes?

Creativity and efficiency

If you don't have time to make your dream a reality, you will have to make time. I often speak to people who throw their hands up at the thought of adding a new project to their lives … I have been there! So where do you find time when you are already stretched to your limits?

The more creative you get with your life, the more you can get done. There are plenty of ways you can create more time in your life. For some people just having a spare evening each week or an extra afternoon free could make all the difference.

What could you do differently each week that will give you some regular time off?

Parents

Swap days off with another family from school. Pick up their kids with your own, bring them home, help with their homework, feed them and take them home in time for bed. The parents of your child's buddy can then return the favour on another day. You both get a guaranteed afternoon and evening clear each week and lots of quality time with your children. Need more days? Swap with two families.

Ask a relative, friend or babysitter to look after the kids while you lock yourself away. If you need more space, head down to the public library or a friend's house.

Employees

Request to reduce your hours in some way — perhaps take a three-day weekend, or leave early once a week. If not, go in to work an hour early each morning and work on your project then.

Can you work from home? If you can save yourself a commute, that could be time spent on your project.

There are myriad other ways of saving yourself time that can be channelled into your project. You need to think outside the box and get creative. Here are a few ideas to get you started:

⇨ Hire someone to clean the house.

⇨ Get more organised and get things done with lightning efficiency.

⇨ Cook several meals or portions at once and freeze them.

⇨ Drop unimportant things.

⇨ Ask others in your household or wider family to take on more responsibility.

Get real about what is important to you. List everything you have to do and then work through the list one by one to see how you could make time for something new.

The million-dollar measure

When I look at how to fit more into my life, I have a way of changing my perspective called 'the million-dollar measure'. Although I am not hugely motivated by money, a carrot as big as a million dollars would definitely pique my interest!

The million-dollar measure is a hypothetical situation where I am offered a million-dollar reward if I am able to achieve something that currently seems impossible.

For example, I am tempted to write a new book, but I just can't see how to fit it into my packed schedule and life. So I look at it from this new perspective: *if* I would receive one million dollars for writing a book in the next three months, would I be able to find or make the time to get the book finished?

The answer is *yes*! The reality is that we generally have far greater physical and mental abilities than we give ourselves credit for, but we are seldom trained to take it to the next level. We are creatures of habit and will only push ourselves to the limits we feel comfortable with.

These limits can disappear, however, when we are faced with certain situations. Mothers have been documented having a burst of adrenalin and enough 'hysterical strength' to lift a car off their injured child. A terminal illness changes people's outlook on life and some will do all the things they never thought possible, to make the most of the time they have left.

In a less dramatic way, meditation, the support of a coach, a personal development course, a relationship break-up or the loss of a job can also shake you up and alter the way you look at the world.

Basically, if you change the way you see the world, you will change what is possible with your time. This may take some creative organisation; it may take asking your friends, family or boss to help while you get things running; or it may take delaying or cancelling other things that you currently spend your time doing. Any which way, there will be some way to make things work for you, and even if there isn't a million dollars at the end of it, making your life-changing dream come true isn't a bad carrot either.

Chapter 10

Money

This chapter is for everyone embarking on a project that will involve some costs. If your project involves falling in love, scoring your dream job or something else with no or very little associated cost, you can skip right onto the next chapter.

The thing about money

Very soon we are going to talk about estimating costs for your project. But before we do I want to talk about money... specifically about the baggage that comes with the idea of money... specifically *your* baggage!

There is no getting away from money. We need it every day to exist in this modern world, but many of us have been trained to look at money a certain way and this view can completely cloud and affect our ability to make, save, spend or use it for the things that are important to us.

Our attitudes to money directly define whether we are wealthy or just getting by. Take a moment to think about your bank balances, your view about money and where that view has gotten you in life.

The main reasons many people have for not fulfilling their dreams are money and time. If you dig deeper still, they will tell you that if they had money they wouldn't have to work, and if they didn't have to work they would be able to work on their dream. As you can see, even reasons related to insufficient time are often in fact all about money.

For the purposes of creating a life-changing project, your attitude to money *will* impact your project in some way. You need to be willing to challenge that attitude as you proceed. For many people that will be life-changing in itself.

For the purpose of realising the goals of your dream project, you need to think of money as a resource that you use to make things happen. Money has a magically fluid way of flowing towards those who are the most creative, positive and persistent about getting it and ebbing from those who are not.

For those of you who, like my husband and I, are starting with limited resources, we will look at ways of creating and growing your project regardless of how much you have to start with.

Desperation

When I set myself a challenge of finding out 'How to Retire in 12 Months', I took a tongue-in-cheek perspective on what was to be a serious challenge.

The challenge was to give myself more freedom from the constraints of working six days a week on my business. I wanted to use the majority of my time for travel, to do the things I am passionate about and to make a difference in the world.

When I was young I had a goal of being a millionaire by the time I was 25. *I failed.*

I have had my fair share of successes and failures along the way, but a few years ago I started to notice a pattern. If my goal is to start a business just to make money, I often fail.

If I start a project or business for the love of it, to reach a personal goal, or to help people, I often succeed and produce much better results than I aim for.

In these situations, opportunities for money just seem to show up without the same sort of grind. I haven't achieved great wealth, but I do get everything I need to make things happen and to live the life I want to live.

The hard times

There was a period a few years back when I had left my job, put all my money in my business and it all failed. I had a lot of debt, was lacking in confidence and often wondered what I was doing. I was still working night and day on my projects, earning very little, and the reality was I started to get desperate.

When I had nothing but debts and bills, my perspective on life narrowed. I could see the light at the end of the tunnel, but it was so far away that I couldn't see any detail. I am a pretty positive person, but I was completely broke, struggled to cover debts and started to exist with a daily level of stress that was very unhealthy.

I was desperate.

I lived in a state of panic and every decision about every cent I spent became hugely important. I would wake up in the middle of the night sweating. My health was bad and I had chronic back pain.

Now I am fortunate I can look back on the periods when I have been desperate, as they are in the past. But some people live like this for years — some for their whole lives.

The problem is that desperation is not conducive to making good decisions, and your poor decisions often send you further down into Struggle Town.

The good times

The good news is I am still here! Now, a few years later, I am in a completely different place, with an income, a great lifestyle and peace of mind.

I made it this far. Why? I think it is because even when things were really tough, I kept on working towards my goals. Even when it seemed to make no sense, I persisted in working towards the life I dreamed of having. Over time things started to change and get better, and with less stress I started to make better decisions.

Eventually the hard work paid off, luck came my way and it all started to work.

My goal was financial but the actual prize was being able to do what I was passionate about, every day. I get to do what I love. I get to make a difference in the world. I get to help other people do what they love for a living.

After a few months of travel my hunger for huge wealth has completely disappeared. If it happens, great! But I do not think about it.

I am interested in having enough money to fund our simple life of travelling and meeting amazing people. I am interested in having enough money so I can enjoy my time with my children (when they arrive). I am very interested in learning about investments and property and 'growing up' financially, but the true goal is to continue to do what I love.

My goal is to continue to set myself challenges and learn and grow and help or inspire other people to do the same. I know that if I continue to look after that, the money will continue to come.

Have a budget

It's time for the good stuff! We need to understand the actual dollars and cents we need to get our projects off the ground.

Regardless of whether you can easily self-fund your project or whether your project requires more money than you think you could possibly have access to, a budget will help you see at a glance what you need to be successful and will help you keep track of costs along the way. If your project will cost $1, $10 or $100 000 more than you anticipated, you want to know that as soon as possible!

There are three main benefits of having a budget. They are:

⇨ understanding what you need

⇨ knowing exactly what you have invested in

⇨ helping you decide which actions need to be taken now or in the future to ensure the ongoing success of your project.

Knowing what you need and how much you're spending helps you avoid many pitfalls and enables you to take action to address any shortfalls — hopefully long before they interrupt your momentum.

Even if you have no idea where the money will come from, to make your project a success you need to have a carefully planned budget that is referred to and updated regularly so that you are on the lookout for opportunities that will fulfil your requirements.

If someone comes to you with an open chequebook, investment, partnership or opportunity, you want to know your numbers straight off. *Note:* an open chequebook seldom happens — but anything is possible!

When you have the money and start spending, make sure you refer back to your budget often: fortnightly, weekly, or even daily if things are happening rapidly. Check that you're on track to help avoid financial surprises.

Five Point Five: budgeting

We created an estimation of costs for the first year and updated it regularly as we discovered more about what we did and didn't need. We talked to a lot of people and asked a lot of questions. This is particularly important if your project (like ours) ventures into unfamiliar territory.

Film gear

We explored digital video recorders, camcorders and DSLR cameras. It took a while to understand the need for light and sound equipment, and even more time to discover what we needed to know about microphones and sound recorders.

We considered that we may have to post footage back for editing, so we factored in the cost of plenty of USB sticks, removable hard drives and shipping.

Also we wanted some way to filter what we had filmed, and we added the cost of editing software and a laptop suitable for editing.

We estimated that this was initially going to cost us $3000.

Services

For the website we thought we would need to hire a developer and pay for graphic design to get a customised look and feel.

We estimated the areas we would need to hire help for would include:

- video editing, to turn the raw footage into the films
- graphic design and website development
- creating our sponsorship proposal.

We were really unsure about the costs for this part, but made an initial estimate of $4000.

Filming

We estimated $400 for general costs for each shoot, mainly in regards to travelling to remote locations; accommodation, meals and potential donations; and costs associated with the charities themselves.

At 12 shoots per year we estimated this would cost $4800 per year.

Marketing

We laid down a general marketing budget of $2000 a year.

Our first estimated budget came to $13 800 for the first year, which then expanded to $16 500 as we learned more about what we needed through research and planning.

Note: When estimating your costs, it's useful to build in a contingency for unforseen costs that you didn't think of at the start — 10 to 20 per cent is a good average. That way, your project is not going to grind to a halt because you left something out that you didn't know was important.

Now it is your turn.

Action: estimate your costs

Download the budget spreadsheet from the website (www.in12months.com/readers — password: success) and customise it to suit your project. If you prefer, you can create your own budget template including the items you need on one axis and the months on the other. Some may be one-off costs and some may be recurring.

Add your estimations and factor in everything you can think of. Update your budget as you do your research and confirm each cost. Here's an example using the sailing trip project example.

	Fundraising materials/ costs ($)	Boat & equipment ($)	Website ($)	Total ($)
January	20	0	10	30
February	0	2500	50	2550
March	0	0	500	500
April	500	1200	0	1700
May	0	0	0	0

Get the money to make your dreams come true

The good news is that the money you need for your project is out there. It really, truly is. The challenge is to make your project exciting enough to the right people to get what you need to go ahead.

First up are the traditional ways that people get money for their big projects: investors, loans and savings. I don't really have anything to add to this that hasn't been said a million times before. As a rule, however, I would look at taking out loans as an absolute last resort. If you can avoid going into debt for your project, then do so.

So how do you get the money you need to make your project a reality? Here are five ways you could potentially find the money you need.

1 Crowdfunding

Crowdfunding is something that has exploded over the past few years. It offers anybody with a great idea the chance to realise it. Crowdfunding, as the name suggests, is the marketing of your idea to a massive network of people, some of whom you hope will be inspired to invest in it. Crowdfunding happens on specialised websites such

as www.kickstarter.com, www.indiegogo.com and www
.pozible.com (AU). There are hundreds of websites that
assist people in getting donations, financial support, loans
or 'in kind' (products and services) that could make your
project viable in the short term.

There are certain types of projects that are more likely to
do well:

🖎 *Projects that are cause-based.* Cause-based projects can
  unite a passionate community of people who want
  to see change. For example, an Australian animal
  rights group wanted to produce a documentary that
  would showcase how pigs are treated in factory farm
  environments. As many people would like to see an
  improvement in conditions for animals, they were
  able to get enough supporters to raise the $10 000 they
  needed to make the documentary a reality.

🖎 *Projects that have great perks or rewards for supporters.*
  Most crowdfunding websites allow project owners to
  create differing levels of rewards to give to people in
  return for their support. Supporters can then decide
  which level of reward they want and pay accordingly.
  Rewards can be great incentives for supporters, so be
  super creative when planning them. For example:

  – Cost out some creative merchandise that will not
    only be a great reward for your supporters but
    could help with your marketing efforts as well.

  – Think about exciting things you could do for
    your biggest supporters; for example, if you
    were a band looking to fund your album, one of
    your rewards could be to play a private gig in a
    supporter's house.

🖎 *Projects that are about creating a new product or design,
  where supporters will receive your new item as a reward.*
  There are many great designs for gadgets, clothes,

jewellery, toys, phones, and so on. In these cases supporters are offered the product, to be shipped once finished and ready for the market, often prior to general release.

When planning a crowdfunding campaign you need to think carefully about how you will market the campaign. A large number of projects go unfunded because the project creator either underestimated how much marketing they would need to do to get the supporters they need, or they overestimated how excited people would be about the cause or the rewards for supporters.

Spend as much time and effort in creating your crowdfunding proposal as you would any business proposition or grant application. You need to take it seriously. Run it by people in the industry, get feedback on your rewards, and go far and wide to find people who would be willing to share it for you.

I am a big fan of this means of sourcing funds so I asked crowdfunding expert Kendall Almerico to share his expertise and to give us his top tips for successful campaigns. Kendall is an attorney and recognised crowdfunding expert. He is a regular columnist on crowdfunding for Entrepreneur.com and *Crowdfund Insider*. These are his seven steps to successful crowdfunding campaigns:

1   *Thoroughly think your project and rewards through.* Look at other similar, successful crowdfunding projects and see what they did. Learn from their successes and use them as inspiration. Have your friends and family review what you plan to do and get their input. Make sure you have a compelling story — something people will care about — and rewards that people will want.

2   *Make a great video.* Good video and audio quality make a difference. You can shoot a good-quality crowdfunding video on your iPhone or with a camcorder, but make sure the lighting is good and

your voice can be heard. Like a journalist telling a story, you want to give the 'who, what, when, where and why'. In addition, give people a reason to get excited and end with 'The Ask' and a thank you. 'The Ask' is where you ask for donations. This should be the last portion of every crowdfunding project video.

3   *List and define your network before you launch.* If you do not have a network of people before you try to crowdfund your project, chances are it is not going to be successful. Crowdfunding projects are not like the baseball field in *Field of Dreams.* Just because you're building it, do not expect that people will come and give you money. You must promote your project to your friends, family, co-workers, social-media networks and everyone you know for it to be successful. Before you launch, go through your Facebook friends, Twitter followers, email lists, phone contacts and anyone else you know. List them all and categorise them so you can market to them appropriately. Your pitch to a family member will be different from your pitch to a person you barely know on Facebook.

4   *Define your core group of supporters and get them ready to donate and help on day 1.* Before you start, list the people you can trust to help you promote your project and who will also contribute without question. These people are your 'core'. Make sure they know what you expect of them before you launch, and make sure they donate to your project on day 1 to give you momentum. Be sure they have whatever they need to be able to promote your project for you.

5   *Research blogs, media and other sources of publicity.* Get the names and contact information for bloggers who may write about your project, and reporters or others who may be willing to provide you with media coverage. Write a short email, or a press release, and have it ready to deliver to them on the day you launch.

6 *Write your posts, tweets and emails and create a schedule to follow.* Before you launch, you should write every Facebook post, tweet and email you plan to send to each segment of your network. Create a schedule so that on every day of your crowdfunding project you know exactly what to post, tweet or send. Having this step out of the way before you start enables you to focus on the things that occur during the project, such as media attention, requests from donors and getting rewards out.

7 *Once you launch, promote, promote, promote!* A crowdfunding project requires a lot of attention and should be treated like a second job. You need to be ready to promote constantly in person, by phone, through email and through social media. You must reach out to media and try to get coverage, and when they say *no*, reach out again. If you are not willing to promote constantly for the duration of the crowdfunding project, do not expect success.

2 Fundraising

If your project is cause-based, charitable or an exciting personal challenge, fundraising is one possible way to get some or all of the money you need. There are so many ways you can raise funds; how you do it really depends on your tastes and creative spirit and the community you have access to.

Tips for fundraising

↬ *Be clear about your target.* How much do you need to make your project a reality? What exactly will you do with the money?

Let people know exactly what they are contributing to and then make sure you do what you say you will do! Unfortunately there are some unscrupulous people who use the proceeds of fundraising to line their pockets.

These people are in the minority, but they have made many people cynical about charity and fundraising projects. For this reason make sure your fundraising efforts are a shining light of integrity and transparency. Be trustworthy and a good role model.

✎ *Know whether donations are tax-deductible (or not).* In some countries, donations to registered charities and not-for-profit organisations are tax-deductible. In these countries a common question you will get is, 'Can you give me a receipt?' or, 'Is this tax-deductible?' It is important that you give people the right information, so do your research first.

If you are working to fundraise for or with a registered charity or not-for-profit organisation and the entire donation will go to them directly, you may be able to provide each person who donates with the option to register their donation individually and get a tax-deductible receipt sent to them from the organisation itself.

If the money people donate will go towards your personal project or to an organisation that is not tax-exempt, then their donation will not be tax-deductible.

To be clear about the status, if you are working with a charity or not-for-profit organisation you should contact the organisation to find out what their tax status is and whether there is a process for official receipts, if required.

✎ *Be clear about what you will do if you don't raise all the money you need.* If you are fundraising for a project and do not succeed, what will you do with what you have collected? Will you contribute the money to a charity? Will you refund the supporters? Think about this before you begin so that people understand what will happen with their money.

✎ *Keep good records.* Keep a record of all donations, preferably with the names and email addresses of those who have contributed.

✎ *Keep in touch.* If people have made a donation, send them an email from time to time to update them on your fundraising progress, and of course on the highlights and progress of your project. Your project will become a representation of all the people who contributed, so don't keep the experience all to yourself!

✎ *Ask people you know to contribute.* This is something that people often skip over because it can feel weird to ask people for money! But the people who know you are usually the people who will be the most keen to see you succeed. So make sure everyone you know is aware of what your goal is and ask if they can help you achieve it in any way. Some people will say *no*, and some people will say *yes* and help you with contributions, ideas for fundraising and plenty of other opportunities.

✎ *Think about the communities you have access to.* Are you part of a knitting, rock climbing or boating club? Are your children in a sports team or do they go to Scouts? Do you meet with a mothers' group or a business association? Do you have a large extended family or a big group of friends?

Your local community is a great place to start when considering what you are going to do. These are the people who can help you make your fundraising event or drive bigger, better and more effective.

People are often very happy to assist with fundraising to benefit a charity or an exciting project, and doing it with the help of others can make it more fun and more successful than doing it on your own.

3 Sponsorship/partnership

Is your project likely to attract a lot of attention? Do you have space that will be visible to the public where you could place sponsor branding or information?

Working with sponsors is an opportunity to get money, partnership, services or products that can either help you get the money you need or cut the costs of making your project real.

Companies will consider sponsorship of projects that will help them achieve their goals. This includes:

🢂 exposure to an audience they can't otherwise reach

🢂 a financial return on their cash investment

🢂 brand affiliation: leveraging cool brands to raise their brand awareness or credibility

🢂 fulfilling their community or corporate social-responsibility goals.

There are many ways you could potentially use your new project to benefit other people's businesses, so be strategic when you are looking for partners and sponsors. Be selective about who you choose. You are putting your partners' and sponsors' names in association with your own, so you want to make sure they are a good fit for your ethos and audience.

Some places where you could potentially showcase your partners and sponsors (by displaying their logos or descriptions of them) include:

🢂 on your website

🢂 on any flyers and posters you have made

🢂 on vehicles related to the project

🢂 in your video credits

🢂 on your social-media backgrounds

⇨ on your merchandise (for example, t-shirts)

⇨ in newsletters (you can mention their business, product/s or service/s)

⇨ in joint press releases.

Basically, anywhere you have your branding is a possible place to display sponsors' and partners' branding too.

> **Five Point Five: our partners and sponsors**
>
> When creating Five Point Five we contacted several companies to find out whether they would be interested in partnering or sponsoring us.
>
> We became blog ambassadors for World Vision Australia and they have helped us visit some of their projects in Latin America. *MiNDFOOD* magazine agreed to be a media partner and share our videos with its web audience. Rode Microphones helped us with sound equipment, Skyrocket Marketing with our website and Adeal with camera accessories.
>
> As we continue growing our project and website our attractiveness to sponsors and partners will likely also continue to increase.

Tips for getting sponsors

Find out if the company you're interested in has a sponsorship strategy. Companies often create an annual sponsorship strategy. They choose the types of companies or projects they want to invest in and what they want the partnerships to deliver.

So before you start creating a sponsorship proposal, ring the company and talk to the sponsorship manager or public relations person to find out if they have a strategy and what they are looking for.

Your questions should include:

- What is your sponsorship strategy?
- What kinds of partnerships do you want to support?
- Do you support sponsorships with cash or in kind (products or services)?
- When should I send the proposal?
- Who should I send the proposal to?
- What kind (and timing) of return on investment are you looking for from your sponsorships?

Once you feel comfortable that you know what the company is looking for from their sponsorship you can start tailoring your proposal so that your project clearly aligns with their goals and time frames.

 Case study: creating a music festival with no money

In 2006 I wanted to create a concert that would promote racial harmony in Sydney. This turned into a festival for 8000 people, but it was only possible with the partnership and support of the general manager of a music venue, Gerard, and the owner of the local community radio station, Russ.

We had volunteers managing every part of the festival, and through Gerard the venue was our key sponsor and partner. As well as providing the venue he used his contacts and relationships to organise marketing and alcohol sponsorship on our behalf.

Meanwhile Russ had festival ads and reads on high rotation on the radio for the months preceding the festival. We had many other partners, sponsors and contributors, but it would not have been as successful or even possible without the partnership and support of these two main sponsors.

---

4 Grants

Grants are essentially gifts of money designed for you to use for the specific purpose outlined in your application. They are usually given to encourage and support certain types of projects or businesses that align with the aims of the donor. There is usually a grant application process where suitable candidates compete for funds.

There are grants for all kinds of projects, businesses and services. Each grant will have a specific set of conditions for the types of projects they wish to fund. Some may be looking for brand-new ideas; others may require you to have had a registered business for years, or a certain turnover or certain achievements. There are a multitude of grants in a multitude of industries, including music and the arts, community, business and sports.

Grants are given by government departments as well as private entities, so it can be very time-consuming to find the right grants for your project. It is also very time-consuming to apply for grants and there is a whole industry of professional proposal drafters competing against you, so if you are going to apply for a grant, make sure you have enough time to do a fantastic job of your application.

5 Marketing campaigns, competitions and popularity contests

With the advent of email marketing and social media a new kind of funding option is now available. Some companies are using their marketing budgets in new ways, and rather than paying for advertising, they create financial or in-kind awards that people can win based on popularity or talent. If you have social-media accounts you have probably been asked to vote for your friends on anything from the cutest baby pictures, to dream jobs, to funding for arts or community prizes.

This kind of marketing is great for the companies involved because they get you to participate in their campaign (and do the work for them). Many of these competitions give the option of voting daily, which means to win you will need to encourage as many people as possible to visit the company's web marketing page as often as possible.

I find that often the organisers of such competitions appear to be looking for free marketing and there is little regard for the people they are recruiting to do the marketing. Some are done very well, but many, despite having a great prize, seem shallow in their intentions.

People who don't win may have worked very hard and annoyed their friends for no result. Those who do win will continue to be used as a marketing tool for the company, with plenty of contracts, potential appearance requirements and more. This may be great news for some people, with even more opportunities to grow your project, and having the backing of a big company may give you instant credibility or weight in your chosen industry.

It is important to read the terms and conditions carefully before entering corporate competitions. If you are going to enter into this kind of engagement you want to make sure you are eligible to win and understand the process and prize before you take time away from your project to rally your voting troops.

Finding the money for your project is a whole project in itself, so don't hesitate to get the ball rolling.

Action: plan the funding for your project

Create a plan to source and secure the funds you need to complete your project. Consider the best funding option for you and your project and give yourself plenty of time to do a great job of it. You may raise all the funds you need with one strategy or you may choose to work on different funding strategies at the same time.

Think through the plan for each method of generating funds and choose one you consider has the most potential.

Chapter 11

Support

If you want to create something life-changing it helps to have support. This is not always so easy to come by! If you are lucky, you may have a family member, friend, teacher or partner who will completely support you from start to finish.

If this happens, *appreciate them*! Many people start the process of designing their lives without any basic support system. If you can create a community of people who support you, impossible goals can immediately seem so much more achievable.

Be prepared to rock the boat

When you stand up and say, 'I am going to attempt to achieve a big goal that will change my life', there is an impact on the people around you, because everyone gets challenged to look at themselves and their lives too.

It is natural that people may not understand why you would want to create change. They may not understand why you choose the goals you have chosen and they may not believe that you are capable of reaching them.

If you are lucky, some people — or even lots of people — will be inspired and stand up with you or support you. Treasure those people! Other people will be inspired but will remain unsure and will sit and wait to see how far you get — although they may never tell you this. These people may confide in you with their opinion years later, or never at all.

Others will feel threatened or challenged, and these are the ones to watch out for. They may seemingly have your best interests at heart, but may try to dissuade you or just be generally negative and unsupportive.

If these people are close to you, important to you or are the people you would expect support from, it can be very disheartening. So you need to understand that even though they may not understand, you must be strong and carry on!

Remember that you are looking to design your life in a world where people very seldom do so. It is not normal to accept responsibility for the fate of your life, chuck out social norms and pursue your dreams. In many cases, you will be considered delusional, especially if you take a long time to reach your goals or if you fail a few times along the way. Of course, once you do succeed you will become inspiring and amazing. People can be a tough audience!

Here is a lighter look at the behaviour of those who are likely to judge you.

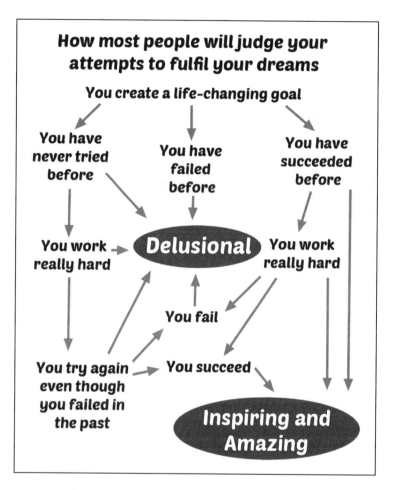

To open the door to freedom, you will have to be willing to shake things up from time to time. You need to be willing to maintain your composure even if you have already failed and no-one believes in you. This actually does make it a little sweeter when you do achieve something exciting because you had the guts to believe in yourself and you were right to do so! You were right to because you do have the power and the motivation to design your life.

I doubt you will ever hear people share that their keys to success were 'to be careful and nice'. Being careful and nice is just not part of the journey to achieving great things in your life, so don't be afraid to rock the boat every once in a while.

Find good people

Finding good people can be a challenge — or not — depending on the kind of person you are. However, if you are keen to create something larger than life as you know it, then having good people on your team can mean you get there more quickly and easily. If it is a family project, a good person could be your partner, a sibling or someone close to you. If you are working on a charity project you may find those good people are already connected with the charity in some way, or inspired by what you want to achieve. I have found people for projects at the pub, on social media, through friends and in job ads!

You never know where you will find the people you need to make your project a success.

Five Point Five: our team

At Five Point Five we started with a team of four people and we agreed that we would build up the foundation of the website. After a couple of months one of the four realised she didn't have the time to make it work, so we became a core team of three: John (filming and editing), Alex (graphic design) and me. Along the way I reconnected with Chris from Skyrocket Marketing, who helped us get our website up and running.

After a while we started to get overwhelmed by the amount of work that needed to be done, so we needed to grow our team. Our first new member was Jen and then we put up a list of available volunteer jobs on our website.

Meanwhile, I met for coffee with a client, Belle, who was looking for a life change. She was about to move to New York and when she heard about what we were doing she was thrilled and joined our team.

Belle brought her expertise in PR and marketing to the team and we started to get radio interviews and magazine stories. This brought more people to the website, and more volunteers with a variety of great skills to contribute started putting up their hands.

This included two editors—Paula and Erika—who gave us a way of managing the additional people wanting to write for us. They both turned out to be excellent and took on more responsibility straight away.

Then Tessa from WP SuperGeek volunteered her services to help us manage the regular needs of our website. At this point we really started to feel we were making progress.

Now as we get more volunteers we can grow what we provide on the website, and we have all sorts of fun people on the team. With all the travel and the lack of internet in many places, we don't have enough time in the day to achieve what we want to achieve. Yet as we increase the size and skills of the team, we are able to grow faster and we have more voices and variety, and it is a lot more fun!

Get coaches and mentors

Good coaches and mentors make life better! When people hear the words 'coach and mentor' they often think of people whose profession it is to coach, or those who are paid to mentor, but I am talking about all the coaches and mentors you will come across in your life and as part of your project, whether you pay them or not. This group of special people may include a parent or family member, a teacher or friend, a boss or colleague or, of course, a life coach, a business coach or a professional mentor.

A coach or a mentor could be any person who makes it a habit to see you as the enormous potential that you are. They are people who can shake you up, ignore your excuses and past failings and reconnect you with your inspiration and confidence, in one conversation.

I have lots of fantastic friends and acquaintances, but when it comes to moral support I confide in just a handful of people with whom I have connected over the years. You may be open to learning from many people, or you may prefer to confide in just a few people, one person or none at all.

If you are in the latter category and have no-one you completely confide in it's time to open up! Coaches and mentors, whether they are paid professionals or people you know, will help you grow faster, learn more and reduce or even eliminate the suffering when times are tough.

They can help you avoid or resolve mistakes and let you know when your internal thoughts are disempowering you, because when it comes to our internal thoughts about ourselves, they often are. If you have no-one you trust to confide in and to approach for support when you are unsure about something, it is probably a sign that you are very uncomfortable being vulnerable. If you allow yourself to be vulnerable you open the door to many more exciting things, such as deeper friendships, more trusting partnerships, love, and of course all the benefits that great coaches and mentors have to offer.

Coaches and mentors may last a lifetime or they may impact you once in a passing conversation. Either way, the more open you are to asking for help, to gaining from others' experience and to being selective about who you learn from, the more likely you are to succeed.

Case study: the importance of mentors

At the age of 16, while attending a personal development course, Catherine Moolenschot realised she loved public speaking. Following the course, she was at an event where the presenter asked her to give a three-minute impromptu speech, which she nervously, but happily, did. A man in the audience was impressed and invited her to speak at a youth event the next day.

Over the next few months she had another six opportunities to speak to an audience, and she loved it. But it wasn't until she went to a speaker showcase and saw paid speakers on stage that she realised she wanted to do it as a profession. Catherine shared with her parents her desire to become a speaker who inspired people, and that she'd decided not to go to university so she could concentrate on her new business.

At first she had no idea how to get new engagements and was naïve about the basics of how the industry worked. Catherine was determined not to let her lack of experience work against her. To make sure she had plenty of opportunities, she attended many events and surrounded herself with people in the industry.

If she met another speaker she offered to buy them a coffee so that she could pick their brains and learn from their experience.

As well as gaining many useful tips, one conversation with a mentor helped Catherine to see that the goals she had set for her business were many times bigger than the goals experienced speakers achieve! Before she learned this she was feeling a quiet sense of failure.

The conversation with this mentor clarified that instead of feeling like a failure, she should feel very proud that she had spoken successfully at so many events in such a short space of time.

Catherine is now focusing on growing her business, and is branching out to speak in the United Kingdom. She still takes every opportunity to learn from various mentors, whether it is through just a single conversation or more regular sessions. See **www.inspiregreatness.com.au**

Surround yourself with like-minded people

A new project generally means taking risks and a lot of trial, error and learning along the way. You will find yourself with new experiences, stresses and problems that you have never faced before. One thing that helps immensely is being surrounded by like-minded people you can learn from.

If you are entering into an unfamiliar world and need to use new technology or solve problems you have never faced before, a network of like-minded people can help you. They will give you a chance to ask questions and to learn from their mistakes and experiences, enabling you to solve problems sooner than if you were trying to fumble through on your own.

Beginners tend to make a lot of the same mistakes and groups tend to learn faster than individuals because they all bring new ideas and solutions to new problems. There are plenty of places you can find like-minded people. Courses are great as they not only teach you the skills you need to get started, but they give you a chance to network and socialise with other people who have the same interests and skill level as you.

You can also meet people at industry and networking events and in forums and communities online. When entering these environments, be vocal! The more involved you get, the more you will get out of it; so contribute, network and ask whatever you need to ask.

Over time you will find yourself naturally being drawn to like-minded people, and you will meet plenty along the way. When you are in the beginning stages of a life-changing project it can feel a little lonely because you are moving out of your normal headspace. This can leave you feeling some what disconnected with your usual friends and networks until you have had a chance to find new like-minded groups and contacts. I am not saying you have to ditch your old friends; you simply need to create new communities, friends and connections as well.

Note: I have created a Facebook group for readers of this book to connect, network and support each other while creating their life-changing projects. Join the group and you will find your first community of like-minded people: www.in12months.com/success-facebook-group.

The importance of partnerships

Partnerships give you the opportunity to expand your reach, effectiveness and credibility significantly faster than you can on your own.

Choose different partners for different reasons — some may have an established community that would benefit from your project, others may have skills or resources that you can exchange for your skills or resources, and others still may share a common ethos or goal that you can achieve together.

As with potential sponsors, look for partners whose values align with the values of your project and who have something that can help take you there. Of course, it is important that partnerships are mutually beneficial to ensure their longevity and the interest of the partners.

Whether you decide to create partnerships, build a team or otherwise collaborate with others, you will need to be effective in the art of leadership and working with people. Most life-changing projects will involve other people in some way, and figuring out how to manage them is a skill you will learn as you go.

How to lead your team

When you are starting out and looking to build a team, the most common problems you will encounter are that people on your team are not as committed, hardworking or reliable as you are. This is very common! It is important to remember that it is unusual for people to fearlessly start something from scratch with no structure, no certainty and no pay cheque. When you find a person or people who match your level of commitment, treasure them.

For everyone else it helps to lead by example, have compassion, and be clear about your expectations. After running several projects I have learned through trial and error that different people need to be led in different ways. Some require constant management and interaction, while others prefer to be left alone to create. Some need to be motivated through their fears and uncertainties; others prefer you to trust them to come up with the goods. Everyone I have met so far appreciates being appreciated, so make sure you do plenty of that!

If you choose to create a team to support your endeavours, make sure you spend enough time with each of them to find out what makes them tick. Find out what you will need to invest in to maximise their contribution and ensure they are satisfied and fulfilled in their role. You will also need to dedicate some time to building cohesion and team spirit between team members, particularly if they do not know each other or have not worked together previously.

This can be tough if you are not all in the same city (or country), as many of my teams end up being. But have no fear! You can use email, private Facebook groups, Google hangouts and Skype to be in communication with multiple people at once and have them feel like they are part of a team. Set up a regular time to communicate and don't let this slide. You can even record conversations using certain tools, so look into what will work for the people who can't be there.

Let's have a look at some types of people and what they can bring to your project.

Creative self-starters: visionaries

These are the big-picture people. They are often self-motivated, excitable and ready with ideas. Creative self-starters are energised by big goals and challenges and can think outside the box when it comes to solving problems or overcoming challenges. Some will be structured and detail-oriented and can take a project from idea to reality; these are often the people who seem to have the most energy and are always working on one project or another. Others are mainly big-picture people who can flit from idea to idea without following through unless they work closely with builders (which I'll talk about shortly).

If you have visionaries on your team it is important they feel they can contribute to the big picture, and it helps if they are able to take responsibility for parts of the project that interest them. If you are a visionary managing other visionaries it is important that you are open-minded and open to contribution. Creative self-starters bring great energy to a team and can hold the vision, even when things are tough. If you are not a visionary but have them on your team it is important you don't dampen the dreamer side, while keeping them focused on the task at hand. Keep your visionaries in the loop about future plans and how you intend to get there, and let them help guide the overall process.

People who need structure: builders

For the majority of us structure is something enforced from a young age. Between home, school and work routines, many people in this world appreciate structure, as they know their boundaries and what is expected of them. They know what the goal is and can achieve it, or not, on any given day, generally depending on how hard they work. Let's call them builders.

A new project has so many unknown quantities that it can make some builders very uncomfortable, because these are people who need clear goals so they can have clear steps to achieving those goals.

Builders like detail. They are task oriented and want to be successful in fulfilling those tasks. They are often the work horses of any team and may or may not come up with the big ideas, but will be the people who ensure the ideas become a reality. They are thorough and can be very hard-working.

If you are visionary and not naturally structured you need to think carefully about how you will look after your builders, because without structure or clear goals, they will feel insecure and uncertain about the project. If the goals are visionary but you do not provide clear and achievable steps to realising them, they will feel inadequate and will often slip away from you and the project.

Ownership: taking responsibility

Ownership is an obscure concept when it comes to new projects. The perfect team member is one who sees the project as their own, even if they didn't come up with the concept, and even if they joined an already established team.

I am not talking about ownership in a financial or legal sense; I mean ownership as the moment when someone decides they will take responsibility for the outcome of a project. If you hire a person for a job, ownership is implied when they agree to your contract. But if someone joins your team as a volunteer, it can take much longer for them to fully own their role in the project.

Different people need different cues before they will take on responsibility. Some people jump into new projects and already feel confident that if they join they want to make it as amazing as it possibly can be. Others will work away, but not feel ownership until they have contributed or until they get some sign that they can really have an impact.

Some people will always feel like they are on the outside, no matter how much they do.

Tips for working with people

Regardless of the types of people you have on your team, here are some tips for making your project run as smoothly as possible:

⇨ *Don't let situations where people disappoint you make you cynical about working with others.* People will probably disappoint you from time to time, and some in a big way. If you fail in this area a lot, look at how you can improve your leadership skills — every part of your life will improve if you can improve your ability to work closely with people to achieve great things.

⇨ *The people you attract are a great measure of the momentum you are creating in the project.* If you get great people jumping on board, you are obviously creating something worthy of their time. If you're not getting great people, have a look at the message you and your projects are projecting — not so much what you say about it, but how other people see it.

⇨ *Deal with problems directly with the people you are having the problems with.* Honesty and a commitment to succeed will solve many issues. Be firm and compassionate.

🖎 *Look at patterns in your team and work out how you are creating them.* If you are having the same problems with multiple people then the common denominator is you.

🖎 *If you have a major dispute or issue with someone in your team, find an unbiased third person to mediate.* Sometimes it's useful to have someone else help you see the situation from each other's perspective. Be open to changing your mind.

Action: consider who you need to work with in order to make your project succeed

List the mentors, coaches, supporters and team members you want and create a plan for securing their involvement, along with a plan for sustaining their participation or support over time.

Approach them one at a time with your concept and see if they would be interested in working with you.

Keep looking for opportunities to expand your team with great people throughout the life of the project.

Chapter 12

Troubleshooting

In the process of chasing any life-changing goal you will without a doubt encounter problems and challenges. It is all part of the journey. This chapter will help you identify issues and find solutions so that you can keep building momentum and moving forward.

As you take action to achieve your exciting new goals, the art of problem solving will become second nature (if it isn't already). It will add a sense of calm when you realise you can solve most of the challenges that are thrown at you, and many of the unsolvable ones won't matter that much anyway.

Seven reasons why your project may fail

Let's face it: your project may fail, but many of the reasons why projects fail are avoidable! If you find that the pathway your project is on seems rocky, this section will help you identify the problems and the changes you can make to get you — and it — back on track.

1 You don't get started

This one is a no-brainer. Just talking about or dreaming about what you want is not enough! Getting started means you are steadily taking actions. If the sum total of your effort is searching the internet and talking to a few people, you will need to lift your game to have any chance of success.

Luckily for us, life-changing projects are created the same way as other projects: one small step at a time. To get results, get started — and then keep going until you get what you are looking for.

2 You lose your commitment

We talked about commitment in chapter 8 and we will talk about it again. Someone who is totally committed will live, sleep and breathe their project. It can be all-consuming at the cost of some other things. Like any big goal in life, the more effort, energy and action you put in the more you will get out of it.

Your commitment may be steadfast or it may waver throughout the process as you encounter challenges and even the possibility of failure. It can be easy to quit something when you think the writing is on the wall. So notice whether you are truly committed or just going through the motions (or avoiding your project altogether).

A lack of commitment based on your fears can have big impacts on your project, so you want to notice as soon as it happens and recommit with all your heart.

3 You lose focus

When you have a big commitment, it can be very easy to lose focus on the everyday stuff that you need to take care of. Losing focus can happen for all sorts of reasons, including feeling overwhelmed, uncertain and fearful.

In my case, I notice that if I take on too many projects or responsibilities I lose focus on all of them. That is my way of sabotaging the results.

Focus is crucial in life because you will get results (good or bad) according to where your attention is — or isn't, as the case may be.

If you find you are not focused on the goal and the final destination, take some time to reacquaint yourself with the goal and the reasons why you want to achieve it. Then look at what actions *will* help you achieve the goal. Minimise all non-essential actions.

4 You let your emotions run the show

Are you an emotional roller-coaster? Are you finding the project is keeping you up at night with panic, uncertainty or worry?

First, this is normal for many people, especially at times when you feel out of your depth or feel that things are not going the way you planned. Second, you need to manage these emotions; they can cause you to do crazy things or get so wrapped up in the emotion that you lose focus and sabotage your project.

Emotion itself is fine. We need emotions to be human. But if you are experiencing a sense of fear or uncertainty to the point that it is causing you to lash out at people, make irrational decisions or struggle to get out of bed, or if you're getting physically unwell, it is time to review how you manage stress.

Creating something from nothing can be stressful. Uncertainty about how your project will turn out can be stressful. Seeing your project fail in ways you didn't anticipate can also be stressful.

Your job is to do the best you can do today. You can choose to live inside the emotion, or you can allow yourself to do everything you can to make your project work. Regardless of the outcome, your ability to manage your emotional responses and persist in the best way you know how will not only give your project the best chance of succeeding, it is also a great way to live in general.

There are two things that tend to stress me out: looming deadlines (such as book deadlines) and the occasional feeling that I have lost my way in a project and that I am wasting time working on things that have no impact. I find my stress shows itself at night, either before I fall asleep or by waking me up in the early hours of the morning. I will have a few hours of panic, sweats and self-doubt. At these times I grab my phone and email myself all sorts of notes and to-do's to review the next morning. My heart races and a rush of creative and sometimes insane thoughts flows through my mind for hours.

This doesn't happen to me very often now, but when it does I find I often wake up the next day with a new level of motivation and clarity about what my next steps will be. In the past, however, it was not such a positive experience.

In poker there is a state of being called being 'on tilt'. Being on tilt usually happens when something does not go your way and you get angry, upset and disappointed at the unfairness of it all. When someone is on tilt they tend to make crazy bets and lose much more money than when they are not on tilt.

With anything big in life, your ability to stay 'zen' (or balanced) when things are tough, or when something bad unexpectedly happens, will help you through the hard bits. Spiritual teacher and writer Eckhart Tolle maintains, 'If you find your here and now intolerable and it makes you unhappy, you have three options: remove yourself from the situation, change it, or accept it totally'.

Anything other than this will create unnecessary suffering, which we do not have time for in the quest for positive life change.

5 You stop believing anything is possible

If you find that the hurdles are all too high, the challenges too many and you are giving up hope, you have probably forgotten that anything is possible. And here is the thing… anything *is* possible!

If anything is possible, what could you create? If anything is possible, what would you do next on your path to success? Believing that anything is possible is a habit you need to build over time. We live in a cynical world with lots of pessimistic and unsatisfied people who do not believe that anything is possible.

The cynicism these people spread can poison you. Even worse, your own self-talk can poison you!

Considering you are the founder and creator of this goal, forgetting that anything is possible will be the beginning of the end. It will not take long for you to prove yourself right and convince yourself that in fact it was not possible after all.

If you notice doubts creeping in or negative or limited conversations coming out of your mouth, you need to reach out, surround yourself with positive people, get some advice from a mentor or advisor, read a book that will inspire you or get some coaching from someone who will help you out of your cynical headspace and back into action.

6 You get scared

This is perfectly normal. Your confidence will grow as you start to see the fruits of your efforts and feel familiar with what you are creating. But fear can be a show stopper if you let it. Fear can:

- limit your willingness to take calculated or intuitive risks
- have you operate in a defensive or survival mode
- make you lose sight of the possibility of the goal

⮑ allow you to quit when things are tough

⮑ affect your ability to make important decisions

⮑ make you crabby, depressed, desperate or mean.

Obviously some of these things will happen to you from time to time, but you need to manage your fear. It also helps to recognise when you are operating *from* a place of fear. Notice your pattern! I find I can't sleep when I am scared of failure. I may wake up in the night or just not be able to get to sleep. This happens to me from time to time when something really important to me is at stake. This is fine. But if it was happening for weeks I would look at what I could do differently, as long-term stress is very bad for your health and your decision-making process.

7 You give up

Apart from not starting at all, all the other reasons for failing are about giving up! Most life-changing projects require a level of persistence and commitment that you may not have displayed before. They require you to do everything it takes to get the result you are looking for — to give more than you have ever given. That is why it is so life-changing: you have pushed through the barriers you have inflicted on yourself.

Quitting or giving up does not fit in that picture! There are a million reasons why you might give up. Some will sound silly and some will sound extremely valid. The more valid your reasons, the more likely it is that you will give up, so don't let those little voices run the show!

The worst thing you can do when you are thinking of giving up is confide in someone who is too afraid to chase their own life-changing goals or someone who doesn't believe in you as an amazing, talented person full of potential. They will accept your reasons as perfectly valid and you will have all the support you need to quit.

It is really important that you surround yourself with enough positivity in the form of supportive friends, family, colleagues and mentors or coaches. Surround yourself with people who will see what is possible even when you do not. These supportive people will help you get through the tough bits when all you want to do is quit, which is great, because giving up on your project is the best way to ensure that it doesn't happen! If you start to feel the need to quit, you need to step outside yourself and analyse why. Look beyond the excuses you are giving yourself and remind yourself why you created this goal in the first place. If you find yourself at this point, go back and read about commitment (in chapter 8) again ... and again!

Sometimes things just go wrong

Although having the right mindset is crucial to success, sometimes things just happen that are enough to stop a project in its tracks, or that subject it to a slow death. Although there are many causes for this, here are seven of the more common reasons why projects don't work out.

1 Your people don't work out

This happens a lot. If you are relying on people to help move your project forward and they don't work out, this can cause trouble for any project or, if there is a major dispute, kill it dead. The people on your team can be your biggest assets but also your biggest liabilities. People are the biggest unknown, as they may get sick, be uncommitted or unreliable, or disagree with the direction you are going in — or who you are as a person.

I have found that as I improve my skills and experience in working with people, I am also better at choosing the right people and I attract those who are more aligned with and committed to my goals.

Your team is a great reflection of who you are being at any given time in your life. But even with the best and most committed people, there is still always a level of uncertainty, because they are not you and they are human!

Knowing this, I am still a big advocate for having a team, partners and taking a risk! Strong partners and keen team members will bring life and excitement to your project. They will encourage and inspire you when you are down, grow the project faster than you could yourself and bring variety, energy and opportunity to the project.

2 You can't get the money

A lack of money and resources can kill a project or make sure it is never born. If you have tried every possible way you can think of, your campaigns have failed and nobody wants to be part of your project, here are some tips for what to do next:

✎ *Don't give up.* These problems are tough for everyone, but the success stories are always the people who persisted even when it looked like there was no hope. Your *yes* is out there! But you need to be willing to persevere to get it.

✎ *Understand what hasn't worked.* You can spend your time quitting and blaming the world for not loving your project, or you can find out why it is not so attractive. There could be a million reasons for this, including:

   – *Your offer was not very exciting.* Analyse what it was that you were offering to people in return for their support. Was your offer realistic? If your promises seem far-fetched, it may turn people off, as would making your offer all about what they can give you (rather than you them). You may not have provided enough information for them to understand what you are doing, or enough passion for them to want to support you. Review everything about your offer, look at how you can do it better and try again

– *You were not clear about what you wanted.* You need to be really clear about how you want people to get involved and you need to make it easy for them to support you. If it is hard for people to figure it out, they are likely to avoid looking further. Be direct about how they can get involved

– *You did not market it to enough of the right people.* Even if your offer is irresistible, if you didn't reach enough of the right people it will fail. Many people underestimate what it takes to promote something successfully. Create a new marketing plan and be creative in multiplying the reach of your market by 10, by 100 or by 1000. Think about who you can incentivise to help you promote it further. Think about who can be a spokesperson and who would be willing to make requests on your behalf or introduce you to new contacts

– *You did not inspire confidence in potential supporters.* When you are not used to it, selling your project to potential supporters can be tough. Sell too hard and you may seem dodgy or annoying. Sell with no confidence in your project and you are likely to be ignored. In addition there are skills you need to learn or outsource to produce professional communications, including:

  o writing emails, sales information pages, brochures, grant applications and sponsorship letters

  o presenting videos

  o crafting posts for social media

  o designing ads.

There will always be room to improve how you communicate with your audience, so get in contact with experts in the field, or at least with people who have had some success with what you are trying to do, and get their honest feedback and suggestions on how you can improve. If you don't know anyone in this field, hire someone to work with you. Being able to inspire potential supporters is something you will benefit from in this project and any others you choose to create in the future, and for most of us, doing it well is a learnt skill.

✎ *Offset your costs.* If you are creative enough, you will find there are many ways to offset your costs, therefore reducing the amount of money you need to get started. As I mentioned in my earlier example, we ran a festival for 8000 people and the only money our team came up with was for T-shirts and to print albums, which we recouped on the night. Everything else financial was looked after by our sponsors, including:

- paying the bands
- everything regarding the venue and staffing
- design and distribution of posters and flyers
- funding and pulling favours for magazine advertising and PR
- the budget for radio reads and marketing.

This kind of relationship can work for any sort of project. If you are planning to sail the world with your family, you may find someone who will give you or lend you a boat in exchange for something (such as the use of your car or house while you are away). You may find sponsors willing to provide you with food products or technology in exchange for video reviews filmed while you are on your journey, or perhaps a logo on your blog or on the boat itself. You could partner with a travel agency, charity or international organisation and agree to speak at events they may hold in certain places you plan to visit. These are just a few ideas, but there will be thousands of possibilities for offsetting costs if you let your creative juices flow.

✏ *Start with something smaller.* If you have done everything you can think of and your project is just not feasible at this moment, start with a smaller project that will lead into your bigger one. Here are some ideas for lead-in projects for the sailing example.

– Produce a website that tracks your journey to making the sailing trip a reality.

– Create a sailing competition (and use it as a fundraiser).

– Connect your sailing club with an organisation for disadvantaged kids so that these kids have a chance to learn to sail.

– Collect stories of people who live on boats with their families, or who have taken extreme voyages, and publish an e-book on Amazon — or contact publishers to find out whether you can work together on the project.

If I sat here for an hour I could probably think of 100 different ideas for a lead-in project that someone could produce in the quest to sail the world with their family. The same goes for any project you wish to undertake. The possibilities are endless.

3 You can't get the audience you need

If your project requires a lot of people to be involved and you can't seem to attract them, this can pose problems, especially if your project is a specific event.

It is important that you take this into consideration before you start planning, as people generally underestimate what it takes to market an event. I can tell you from experience that it is not a good feeling when nobody shows up!

Depending on the type of project you are embarking on, you will need to attract people in different ways. For example, getting more people to visit a website to sign a petition would be a different process from getting people to the launch of an exhibition, and different again when engaging schools in a project.

I won't go into too much detail here, as this topic requires its own book! But I have included some brief tips along with some universal ideals for marketing your project if you have more time.

Last-minute tips for getting more people

So, you are getting close to your event and you have a sneaky suspicion that unless you create some magic you are going to find yourself with fewer people than you want/need for the event to be a success. Here are some tips for marketing to the masses at the very last minute:

➯ Call local radio stations to see if they will interview you or broadcast your event details.

➯ If it is a local event visit the local shops in the area, tell them about the event and invite them. If you have time, print flyers and ask if they will keep your flyers on the counter or, better still, give them to people when they make a purchase.

➯ Contact every person you know and ask them to bring their friends and promote it through social media.

➯ If it is a ticketed event, offer some tickets as giveaways to relevant bloggers if they can promote the event to their databases.

➯ Call everyone who has been involved, even if only remotely, to see how they can promote it to their audiences.

Essentials for your marketing plan

Hopefully you are reading this before you begin so that you can give yourself plenty of time to execute a fantastic marketing plan. If so, here are some essentials that should be part of your marketing plan:

➪ *Partner with communities.* When looking for the people you want to reach, it is important to consider the other communities they socialise, congregate and communicate with. If you can engage an established community of 20, 200 or 20 000 you will be far better off than doing it alone. And there is no reason why you should stop at one! Aim to work with a variety of complementary communities if possible.

➪ *Contact relevant publications for media partnership.* Are you a big fan of a certain magazine that would be a great fit for your story? Depending on your event, there are all manner of ways you can involve a media organisation in the event itself or the journey to it. They may do a single story or several as your project unfolds. They may allow you to guest blog on a regular basis. There are many exciting ways you could work with media partners. Think about how you can help them get great, relevant content for their audience.

➪ *Keep your stakeholders updated.* Regularly email everyone who has agreed to help promote your project with updated information, briefs, tweets, images and posts that they can copy and paste when they are scheduling their marketing.

➪ *Subscribe to* www.sourcebottle.com *and look for PR call-outs* relevant to your project. Depending on your project, you may find opportunities a few times a week. When responding to call-outs don't just copy and paste your blurb or send a press release. Read the call-out carefully and write a detailed response with your story and why it relates to what they are looking for. If you want to send a press release as well, that is fine, but make sure your written response gives them everything they need.

✍ *Build a database.* A database can be your biggest asset for this and subsequent projects. With tools such as Mailchimp (www.mailchimp.com) you can set up a subscription form that you can link to from any of your marketing materials, including your website (if you have one). Likewise, you can run competitions where people subscribe with a certain link. If you collect lists offline, enter them immediately and send a group email to welcome them. Make sure you email your database at least once a month to keep them up to date with the project.

4 Your project is stopped

So you were cruising along fine and then something happened that destroyed your momentum. Maybe a member of the team or an important partner pulled out. Maybe you found a legal regulation that means your original idea is not legally possible. Maybe you realised that you need something that you just can't seem to get.

A few of my projects have gotten stumped for all sorts of reasons. This happens a lot in life, especially when you are inexperienced at the game. When your project gets stopped unexpectedly, especially when it is dramatic, it can be very disheartening and seem the perfect reason to give up, especially if it was hard at that time.

These situations can be very stressful and it is hugely important that you, as the leader of a project, don't let your team see this as a reason to give up. Most situations have an alternative solution that needs a clear, creative head to figure out. And even if it doesn't seem ideal at the time you can make an even better project than you originally aimed for. Things *do* happen and the key to success is to be flexible, creative and keen to succeed despite any seemingly enormous challenges that spring up along the way.

 Case study: overcoming all challenges to family travel

Tracey Pederson was ready for something new and exciting, but she was reluctant to leave her good income and company car. She had grown up thinking that once she got a company car she would be happy—that it was proof she had made it. For 18 months, even with the car, she was not happy. However, she had no idea what to do next.

One day, on a work trip, her flight was delayed and she was stuck at the airport all day. She bought some motivational books, and by the time she got home she had made the decision to leave Australia with her family to travel the United States for 12 months.

After a couple of days of working out the numbers, she had a plan and her husband, Gert, was on board. They gave themselves six months to generate the money they needed. This included careful saving, selling almost everything they owned, and various other little projects.

Challenge 1: Get a 12-month US visa. They found out US tourist visas were only valid for a maximum of six months—this was only half the time they needed.

The solution they came up with was to open up their itinerary to include Europe and Asia. It was a big change to the vision they had for the trip, but to have a year away they needed to be creative in how they could make it a reality.

Challenge 2: Sort out the children's schooling. The second challenge saw Tracey spend months researching home schooling, distance education and more, but it seemed that nothing was going to work for their situation. They could not

(continued)

Case study: overcoming all challenges to family travel *(cont'd)*

see how they could take the trip without holding one of their daughters back. Finally, with only weeks to go, they found a state exemption that suited their daughter's needs in high school. They had the school principal sign it and she was able to skip a year without being penalised.

As a family, they had a fantastic 12-month adventure with life-changing experiences, and the children had the opportunity to see the world. As a family, they spent more time together than they ever had before and after their initial concerns they now have an incredible bond and a family dynamic that was not present before the trip.

On her return to Australia, Tracey was determined not to get trapped in a 'normal' job again. The trip had opened her eyes to many opportunities and so they devised a new plan. They were offered an opportunity to rent a house in Malaysia and sublet it until they were ready to move there. Meanwhile, while Gert was back at work, Tracey started taking freelance writing jobs and building her income potential online.

When I last spoke to Tracey she and her family had based themselves in Malaysia, with lots of travel every three months while they build up their income streams and plan the next exciting move. Tracey documents her journey at **www.lifechangingyear.com**

5 Your project changes direction

Projects change … a lot. Especially if your project runs for several months or years. This is a normal experience as you open the door to new opportunities and bring in new people with their experiences, dreams and contacts.

Part of the excitement is that you don't know how it will turn out. It is important that you are flexible about how your goal will be fulfilled, as you are much more likely to achieve success if you are open-minded about how you achieve it.

Keeping this in mind, it is important to know what you will and won't compromise on. For some projects you will be keen to chase all opportunities, with the mindset of 'the more, the merrier'. For other projects, you may have a specific path you wish to take, even if fantastic opportunities come along that you have to turn down. It is important that you choose opportunities that fit your values, and this can cause some serious discussions in a team environment!

It helps to establish these values early on within your team so that you are clear about what you are all aiming towards, although this can often be overlooked.

Five Point Five: how plans change

At the moment John and I have been working with rough plans for up to three years in advance. We plan the continents we will be visiting and go from there. Every six months or so we review our travel plans to see if we are still happy for things to happen the way we planned them. Originally, we were to spend 12 months in Latin America—which turned into 20 months as there was so much to see.

We get a lot of opportunities along the way (such as writing this book), and these things help mould the plan. Instead of heading straight to Asia after Latin America we decided to spend eight months writing and visiting family and friends in Australasia and Europe before the next leg of our official travel. Our original plan was three years of travel and then start a family—but our travel plan now looks more like a possible four and a half years! Instead of worrying that we will be too old to have babies, we have just decided to review our plan each year.

(continued)

Five Point Five: how plans change *(cont'd)*

Meanwhile we found so many amazing artisans on our travels and have a passion for healthy travel products, so we are excited to be launching a shop on the website. This is an opportunity that came out of the project itself rather than something that was in the original plan.

We have a clear understanding of our core goals and the rest is open to considering all the fantastic opportunities that come up along the way.

Chapter 13

Resources

Depending on the type of person you are, your life-changing project may require you to be a lot more organised than you have been in the past.

There is a huge number of very cool tools and resources you can use that will help you get organised, save you time, help you communicate or give you a professional image. Here are some of my all-time favourites:

- *Project management.* I have used several project-management tools, but it wasn't until I started using Basecamp that it all made sense! The interface is very easy to use, and your whole team can see exactly where you are regarding each part of the project. It helps with to-do lists in real time and you can upload all your associated documents. This is an awesome tool that will help you manage all of your projects and you can use it for $30 a month.

- *Get professional.* Some of your projects will require you to put yourself out there. In these cases it helps if you can create a functional website and a professional-looking email account. Websites do not need to be expensive to look good and be useful! I recommend www.wordpress.org (not to be confused with wordpress.com) because it is scalable, completely flexible and can grow with your website. It is a free, open-source application, but you do have to pay for hosting and for a domain name.

I run a course that teaches people how to create their first website and most people are surprised that they are able to create a professional-looking website themselves. There are hundreds of different ways to create a website, and it can be overwhelming to figure out what to do.

I won't go into too much detail on websites in this book, but if you need more help on this topic go to www.grassrootsinternetstrategy.com.au or check out the Website Launchpad course at www.in12months.com/website-launchpad.

If you need a professional email address, you can buy the domain you want through a domain host and link it to an email management tool such as ZohoMail (www.zoho.com/mail/). ZohoMail is free and gives you a web client for your emails that you can access from any computer and/or synchronise with your phone or laptop directly. This way you get a professional domain and email addresses. For example, I created my email address, serena@in12months.com, using this process.

✑ *Back up your life.* Backing up is something many people are very bad at! It's not until you lose something you spent a lot of time on that you start to take it seriously.

I don't just mean backing up your computer; I mean backing up your life. Backing up your life saves you much time and pain when you lose something such as a password, phone, laptop, website or, at some point, your life!

I use a few different tools that give me better security for the things that are important to me online.

Dropbox (dropbox.com) is now the main folder on my laptop. Inside are all the documents, photos and files that I have saved for my business, projects and personal life. As soon as I am connected online, Dropbox gets busy in the background updating the server with all the changes and new files and photos on my computer. If by some chance my laptop stops working, gets stolen or falls in the ocean, I can still access everything mirrored on the Dropbox folder from any computer. It is also a great way to share files with other people on my various teams. It is free for small users, and costs from $100 per year if you have a lot to back up.

ManageWP (www.managewp.com) is a management tool for WordPress that I use as the base for my websites. I love ManageWP because I can manage the technical aspects of my website, in particular backups and updates. I am not a technical person and this keeps my websites secure without having to pay people to keep an eye on them. As well as everything else, it runs backups automatically and then saves them to Dropbox.

Roboform (Roboform.com) is a password management tool that remembers the hundreds of passwords that we seem to need these days. It just runs in the background and saves each new password as I create it. If I ever need to find a password from an obscure website, I just click open Roboform and it shows me the login details and fills in all the fields for me. A licence is about $20 a year and Roboform is accessible from anywhere, so if I lose my laptop I still have all my passwords (phew!).

⇨ *Communicate.* For many people, designing their lives may require communicating on a whole new level. There are some fantastic tools such as Skype, Facetime, Viber and Google Hangout that enable you to talk to people all over the world for free. There is no reason why you can't contact people as long as you have a smart phone or access to a computer. These days most people are hyperconnected, and you will find many well-known people are available and responsive on Twitter.

The World Clock Meeting Planner (www.timeanddate .com/worldclock/meeting.html) is a handy, free web tool that will help you plan appropriate times to speak internationally with your contacts.

⇨ *Save time.* We talked about saving time and prioritising and there is a huge number of people, tools and resources available to help with this.

Unroll (www.unroll.me) is a free email application that manages all your email subscriptions in one place. Instead of dozens of emails from different people, you will get one email that displays all of your newsletters in one place.

Freelancers and virtual assistants can expand many areas of your project, looking after things you need done to save you time — writing, providing graphic design or editing video or text, contacting people on your behalf and much more. Basically, you can pretty much outsource anything you don't need to do yourself. There are websites such as Elance (www.elance.com) that will give you access to thousands of freelancers. You simply post the job you have — big or small — and people will apply with samples of their work and a quote. You go through each proposal and decide which freelancer you want to work with. If you are on a very tight budget there are websites such as Fiverr (www.fiverr.com) where people can post specific jobs they will do for a set fee, often just $5. This is especially useful for small, creative jobs.

Like any employment situation, it can be a little hit-and-miss when working with new people, especially if you are not paying much! With any new project, you need to balance your needs with your budget; sometimes it is worth paying extra if you know you will get a good-quality product or freelancer.

Over the years I have worked with many fantastic freelancers, virtual assistants and service providers and am often asked for recommendations. I have collected a list of those I work with and refer my clients to. You can find them here: www.in12months.com/success-resources.

☞ *Collect money.* Will your project require you to fundraise, sell goods/services or collect money? There are tools and applications that will help you with this, the most common being PayPal (www.paypal.com). Paypal is an online payment system that buyers can connect to their bank account or credit card, giving them constant access to funds for online transactions.

Sellers can email PayPal invoices or accept payments through their website using PayPal widgets or buttons. You can also connect PayPal to other e-commerce applications for the management of the financial side of the transaction. A cool new PayPal offering is a device that connects to your mobile device and allows you to swipe credit cards. This can be a real help if you are running events, and for other point-of-sale purposes. It's worth noting these tips about PayPal.

- *Tip 1:* When setting up PayPal for your new project, ensure the name you use is the same as that recorded on your bank account. If you use a different name, you will not be able to retrieve the funds.

- *Tip 2:* When adding PayPal buttons to your website do not use the 'Donate' buttons unless you are a registered charity. You can still ask for donations; just don't use the donation button because if you do you will not be able to remove the money from PayPal without proving you are a real charity.

- *Tip 3:* As with any financial application, test it properly before launching it for external use.

✑ *Broadcast.* Does your project require you to get a message out there? Will you be running a course or a group conversation, or broadcasting a presentation? Will you be interviewing someone? Does your project need people to learn about you, your cause or your project?

There are many reasons why you may need to understand how to broadcast your message or communicate with a large group of people.

GoToWebinar (www.go2webinar.com) is not cheap at $99 per month, but it is the best tool for online, real-time group presentations, courses and webinars. Google Hangouts (www.google.com/hangouts) is a free live option for up to nine people. You can also broadcast your video live to YouTube (www.youtube.com), which is a pretty cool feature for live shows. Facebook and Twitter are places where you can connect with an audience of like-minded people, and Facebook groups enable you to have group conversations openly or in private.

A blog or website also gives you a place where interested people can follow your progress in detail and be part of your community.

Chapter 14

Our 12-month diary

A lot can happen in 12 months, even if you have very little time to pack in extra stuff! This is the timeline of the first 12 months of our project, Five Point Five, which, as you will see, included plenty of ups and downs.

I have included this here so you can see that it is never plain sailing when you start a life-changing project. It doesn't matter how shiny someone's efforts look from the outside, there are always ups and downs when creating something from nothing. For us, the experience was mainly exciting and positive. But it was intense, hard work and sometimes exhausting at the same time!

Month 1

We are living in a cute apartment in Bondi Beach, Sydney. I manage my small business from home and John manages a bar. We have return tickets booked to Venezuela and as we prepare to leave we get inspired to start the as-yet unnamed Five Point Five project. With only weeks to go, we have to get into action! Our milestone this month is to find sponsors and partners before we leave, so I create a list of potential organisations we would like to work with. We submit proposals for:

➭ the gear we need (in-kind sponsorship)

➭ cash sponsorship

➭ help with editing videos

➭ potential media partners to help us promote the videos.

I make 10 calls or applications a day as we are short on time. It takes a lot of time to do the research on each company's sponsorship program, and they each want the application in a different format.

The first result is from a client who calls out of the blue. His boss has agreed to provide us with a tripod and camera bag. We are thrilled and touched that people are working behind the scenes to help us — a huge benefit of having made a public declaration. Then we get a call back from Rode Microphones. They will help us with our video microphones and accessories. We did not know at the time just how crucial this gear would be to the quality of our videos.

Meanwhile, we have not heard back about any other sponsorship proposals. We knew it was short notice when we started, but after following the rest up and getting *no*'s or silence we decide we will approach sponsors again once we have the website up and something tangible to show them.

We ask two friends if they would like to be on our core team and they both say *yes!* Bonus! We are now a team of four. We agree to each write once a week for the first year to build the foundation for the website.

We connect with World Vision Australia and they love the concept and want us to be blog ambassadors. They have plenty of projects in Latin America so we will get to make our documentaries for their projects too.

Meanwhile, we are packing up our apartment, and selling or giving away everything that we own. I consolidate my office onto my laptop and John is working up to the end. It is a super stressful month and we are not sure if we will make it, or if we are ready! We have many thoughts about delaying our flights to give us more time, and to give John a chance to save some more money before we leave.

We stick to the date and the day before we fly out *MiNDFOOD* magazine get in touch. They like the concept and are keen to post our videos on their website … we have a media partner! We learn that:

➪ it is never too early to start contacting potential sponsors and partners. It taught us a huge amount about how the process works, and a few great organisations got involved.

➪ sometimes it pays to stick to your original dates, even if things don't look good. You can get miraculous amounts done when you are close to the deadline.

➪ the more we talk about the project, the more opportunities open up. Word of mouth is already spreading and we haven't technically done anything yet.

Month 2

Goodbye, Australia!

We arrive in Caracas and spend some time getting used to the climate, language and intense culture. Then we head out to the coast and start to relax and get into the groove of travel.

This month we go through our plans and ideas. We dabble in some writing, ready for when the website is up. We practise using our new gear and film two video blogs (we plan to post weekly video blogs throughout the journey).

John's goal this month is to learn how to use the video editing program Premier Pro. He does this by watching hundreds of YouTube tutorial videos and reading tips on forums. He finds it very frustrating to learn, but is thrilled when things work.

We have our first work-related argument. We now work, travel, adventure, socialise and spend every single moment together — luckily we are both quite relaxed, or it could be a rocky road.

After staying in a few places we decide that video reviews of places and accommodation would be helpful to other travellers, so we film a trial one to see what we can produce.

Meanwhile, I am concerned about finding community projects for our documentaries and worried the communities will find it intrusive if we film their work. We do some research online and find one in the slums of Colombia. We email them, they are keen and we book it in.

This month we really just do things ad hoc. We don't have any rhythm or structure yet and we are busy enjoying our travel and new-found freedom. We learn that:

➾ sometimes you have to realise that part of making things work is to find a natural rhythm, especially when you are in unfamiliar territory

➾ the only way to find out if someone is interested in working with you is to ask them.

Month 3

We cross the border into Colombia and head to a little charity called Fundación Mariposas Amarillas (Yellow Butterflies Foundation), where we will volunteer for three weeks and film our first mini-documentary. The charity is made up of two little schools that the founder, Oscar, has set up to look after kids who have no access to school otherwise.

It is quickly apparent that our lack of Spanish is going to be a problem, as we can't even speak to Oscar.

The night before, I am almost sick with nerves. I am terrified of public speaking and I hated school when I was young, so teaching is not something I have ever considered doing!

Of course, it was much better than I feared! Although they are gorgeous, volunteering with the kids is quite intense because we speak different languages. Luckily there are other volunteers who are fluent in both English and Spanish and they really help us by translating in school and in our interviews.

We realise that volunteering and filming at the same time doesn't work, and decide that in future we will do one or the other.

We write a proposal to review hotels and send it out to a few in the area. We book our first two and the learning curve is huge, but the owners are great to work with and the places we stay at are lovely.

One of our team of four realises that she can't commit the time anymore and the other is about to have a baby and disappears. So it is just John and me working on the project for now. It is sad to lose people so early in the project.

We learn that the risks we have taken to get to this point are starting to pay off. We are starting to see what our dream life will really feel like and it is an amazing thing.

Month 4

We get an unplanned extra two weeks in Cartagena and decide to visit some hotels and hostels in person to ask who would like us to review them. At the first one we go to we meet the owner, who is keen for a review and can help us book a sailing trip to Panama.

He also has a new travel company in Panama City, so we agree to review one of his tours there too. Our sailing trip is amazing and we film it so we can practise filming tours. We regret not filming the trek we just did to The Lost City. We have time to review one more hotel in the north of Panama before we set off for Costa Rica.

We speak to several people along the way who love what we are doing and want to write for us, but we are not able to do anything with them yet so they drop away. The website is in progress, but it is very slow and I start to feel the pressure, as we have promised people it would be up by now.

We are so focused on the videos and travel that other things slide. We are getting some great filming opportunities, so things are very positive; we are just not achieving everything we plan for each month, so we agree that what we do achieve is fine for now because one of our goals is to enjoy our travels.

We learn that there are so many opportunities waiting for those who dare to make requests. The more you share your project, the better. Every conversation is an opportunity to have something exciting happen.

Month 5

We volunteer for Endangered Wildlife Trust, a leatherback turtle conservation project in Costa Rica, and halfway through we decide to film it for our project too. So far we have been lucky to find volunteer translators who are friends of our interview subjects. Without them it would be impossible at this point for us to tell their stories! Even with the translations, John is finding it very difficult to organise the stories and do the subtitles. But it is great practice for his Spanish.

We get in contact with an organisation in Nicaragua that supports grassroots women's projects around Central America. We head off to film a group that fought for the right to set up a women's football league in Ometepe called

Amojo. To get the story we travel for hours by 4×4 on insane rocky dirt tracks to a remote village at the foot of the volcano.

The website is still a work in progress and it is not ready to see the world. We have started a Facebook page and are using that to communicate with people about the project until the website is ready. I am almost nervous about having the website go live because in the beginning it will be so empty. It is a juggling act travelling and running three websites while setting up a fourth. The weekly video blogs we planned never got past the first two. Maybe we will start them again sometime soon.

We review a surf hotel on the Pacific coast and the place is breathtaking. At this point we are starting to get used to this new way of life. We are still pinching ourselves each day — yes, it *is* real! We learn that:

- we are living the dream! Our days are packed with adventure and we are having incredible experiences off the beaten track.

- when you start to get momentum everything becomes a little easier to manage — things just seem to fall into place.

Month 6

We head up to the north of Nicaragua to film a group of women who were sex workers in the past. Their group is called Las Golondrinas. They now work to educate sex workers in the area about health and their basic human rights. We spend a day driving in the back of a truck with these women. They take us to a brothel and share their stories with us. The level of poverty, violence, discrimination and hardship is almost overwhelming. Today is the first day we really feel like journalists and we are amazed at how quickly you can connect with people when you don't speak the same language.

One of our goals this month is to promote Five Point Five by writing for other websites and having them share our videos. Website owners seem keen, but getting it to the next step with them is proving to be a long, slow process. We are like a little plankton trying to get the attention of dolphins and sharks — it's tough, but we persist!

We head to Utila in Honduras for three weeks to work on the business and do some diving. We have been neglecting our other projects in favour of Five Point Five, so we need to do some maintenance and catch up.

With all the work we're doing, the website is still not up. It is starting to be a running joke between us, but it's not really funny.

We learn that sometimes you just have to be patient and accept that you can only do so much in a day.

Month 7

We spend a week learning Spanish in Antigua, Guatemala, and realise that we should really spend a month: it helps so much! But we already have hotels to review in Lake Atitlan. Unlike previous countries, we haven't arrived with community projects booked for Guatemala so we hope we will find some good ones along the way.

At Lake Atitlan we find two great projects to film; Amigos de Santa Cruz and Konojel, both helping the Mayan communities who now live in tiny, isolated communities. Meanwhile we do our hotel reviews and hit it off with a lovely couple who ask us to stay longer and even offer us a house to stay in! It is with heavy hearts we push on as we have flights booked from Mexico and we need to get there.

At Lake Atitlan the internet leaves a lot to be desired. In one town we find that the connection dies when it rains — and it is the rainy season! We start to crave wi-fi and our project goals are falling behind. At the same time we get contacted twice by media people interested in our story.

But it is so peaceful and beautiful here it is hard not to relax and enjoy the serenity of the place. It is a new kind of roller-coaster. We learn that:

➯ as we grow more confident in producing films, we are able to go deeper with our interviews and are getting more from each story

➯ we are getting wonderful and emotional responses from the subjects of our films. We are beginning to understand that our videos are an acknowledgement of everything they do.

➯ even if some goals fall behind, your momentum can create exciting advances behind the scenes.

Month 8

We move to the east of Guatemala to film an orphanage in the jungle called Casa Guatemala. The orphanage and school look after 300 children and provide them with regular meals and an education. They are struggling to survive financially and we hope they can continue to do this important work. One of their many success stories is an orphan who is now finishing his medical degree in Cuba. We take his details so we can interview him there.

As well as the normal documentary, John also whips up a quick film for a travel film competition. He only has 24 hours to film and edit it and send off his entry. Meanwhile, he is interviewed from Ireland on radio and in two papers about his story and I am interviewed from Australia. We are thrilled with the sudden interest, all of a which seems to have come from word of mouth.

My sister gets married in New Zealand this month and I am gutted not to be there. This is one of the downsides of being so far away. I am in the jungle in Guatemala when she says her vows.

We have a set date for flights and we end up rushing through Guatemala. We cross through to Belize and finally after two months of internet problems we get a good connection and attempt to catch up on websites, businesses, projects and all my clients on Skype. It is not until we get to Belize that we learn that Skype is banned there. We make do with what's available while enjoying some incredible diving and snorkelling.

After a week in Caye Caulker we scoot through the Yucatan Peninsula of Mexico, promising ourselves we will spend more time there when we return from Cuba.

The website is up; imperfect as it is, it is up! It is terrible timing as we are travelling in Cuba and now we will have almost no internet for a month and can't promote it or fix it up in any way — but still, it is up! We learn that:

⇨ travelling through remote parts of the world while relying on the internet is very frustrating!

⇨ having an 80-per-cent-there website is better than no website at all. We can always fix things along the way but something is definitely better than nothing.

Month 9

We buy 30 minutes of internet after a few days in Havana and find out that we are listed as a finalist in the video competition! Considering we have only just learned how to do all this it is an exciting reminder that we are on the right track.

We also have no response from the young medical student from the orphanage, Axel. We email the director of the orphanage to see if she has other details for him, and head off to travel around Cuba.

Cuba is amazing and after the buzz of Havana, the gorgeous calm of the beaches and the adventure of the south, we regroup and set ourselves new goals. I feel inspired and start this book and write plenty of blogs. Cuba is the most inspiring place we have been to.

When we get back to Havana we still have not heard from Axel. The response from the orphanage is to try the local hospital, so we find ourselves on a hospital adventure! There are many hospitals in Havana and finally, three days before we leave the country, a security guard takes the time to understand us and gives us the phone number for the student residences. Two more days of frustrating conversations in fast, thick Cuban Spanish and suddenly we have Axel on the phone. He will come to meet us on our last day there.

One of our personal goals was to be able to have a conversation in Spanish by the time we reached Cuba. John's confidence has him speaking Spanish long before I do; he is even cracking jokes! But it is still a huge joint effort for us to understand and be understood in the context of interviews. We learn that:

➪ when you are in the thick of a project it sometimes pays to take a good break from it. It frees your mind to look at it from a new perspective, and you come back to it renewed.

➪ if Cuba had better internet access we would live there. Our new favourite country … hands down!

Month 10

We head back to Mexico (and internet!) and this month we review more hotels and visit a bee conservation project Melipona Maya, that is protecting a Mayan species with only an estimated 100 hives left, and a sustainability project in the same village.

We travel 24 hours by bus to film another project in a remote village. This time it's the work of major charity World Vision. After a day to recover we take another 12-hour journey to Mexico City where we visit another World Vision project. We meet a former sponsored child, Carolina, who is in her last year at university.

This month feels like a blur, as we travel such long distances. We get a chance to post a batch of review videos, and the hotels respond enthusiastically. They are thrilled with what we have created. This is great for our confidence!

At this point we stop for a couple of weeks and enjoy a quiet Christmas in Mexico City. We learn that:

> we love the variety in our new way of life. No two days are the same! It doesn't feel like work, and we are living like we have never lived before.

> too much travelling can take it out of you. Mexico is a lot bigger than it looks on the map.

Month 11

This month, as well as doing a lot of travel, we are spending our time working on getting the website to the next level. Our to-do list is enormous and we are behind in everything, but life is good at the same time!

Over the past couple of months we have travelled and experienced so much! It is fun, but exhausting, and it has been very tough achieving our website goals at the same time. We decide that next year we will stop every two to three months to catch up, regroup and attempt some normality.

We say goodbye to Latin America for three months and head to San Francisco to stay with John's brother and sister-in-law. We are very excited about the fast internet! We upgrade some of our camera gear, a laptop and other things to make our lives easier.

We get our first proper volunteers on the team: an editor and a writer. We are thrilled! With a desk, internet and a great working space we are able to get the website back on track. I run a course and can have an open schedule for my coaching clients.

Here we clear our heads and set up structures for the business, including schedules for social media. We start to review how things have gone, and plan for the next 12 months. We look at all the opportunities available to us now as a result of the work we have done. It is exciting! We learn that:

⇨ you need to be prepared for people to join your team, especially volunteers. It is important that you have enough time to look after them.

⇨ it is important to celebrate the wins! We get so tied up in what we haven't done yet that we forget how much we have achieved.

Month 12

We are settled after being in one place for so long. We send out our first email to our database, get our new Volunteering Overseas e-book up on the website and lots of people download it. The e-book is even shared on a major website with good reviews; the work has all been worth it.

Meanwhile, I have been contacted by a writer to be interviewed for a volunteering book she is publishing in the United States. She even wants some photos for the book. We are approached by three different companies about products they want us to review on the website, which means we are starting to be found in their Google searches.

We start a podcast. It is lots of fun and so perfect for us, but we end up sidelining it until we have more time and people involved in the project.

With all the new momentum, three volunteers put their hands up and start working with us. This is very exciting because they see our project as something they want to be involved in. We start to plan the second stage of our trip: eight months travelling down the west coast of South America. This is the place I have been dreaming of for so many years. We create a plan to add tours and cruises to the types of companies we review and look at how we will expand the offering on the website, including our initial plans for a travel health shop.

We now feel like seasoned travellers and have an incredible sense of freedom. We were happy with our lives in Sydney, but the past year has been enlightening, exciting and relaxing all at the same time! Not only are our lives physically different, but I *feel* different too. I am living with more confidence, compassion and peace than I have ever experienced. The relationship John and I had was close and loving before, but now we are an unstoppable team as well. We learn that:

➪ stability does make you more productive!

➪ once you have momentum it is so much easier to follow a new opportunity. Your previous effort not only impacts that project but every project that comes in the future.

*   *   *

As you can see, a lot can happen in 12 months! Our 12 months were very exciting and challenging.

Your project may look like this or look very different. There is no right way to go about things; just put one foot in front of the other. If you are likely to get caught up, think about reviewing your project this way as well. It only needs to take an hour at the end of each month to look at what you have achieved and learned, and what you could do better next month.

Chapter 15

Wrapping up and moving on

You set yourself a goal that has the potential to be life-changing. Whether you succeed or fail, it helps to evaluate the result so you can learn from what did and didn't work. Regardless of the outcome, you want to tie up all the loose ends so you can start with a clean slate for the next project.

Sometimes we can carry over emotional baggage, such as guilt, a sense of failure, uncertainty or arrogance and overconfidence from one project to another, whether it succeeds or fails. This is normal, but it can taint your new project. Bring learnings, experience, confidence, motivation and positive anticipation — and leave the rest behind.

Here are some questions to ask at the end of each project or attempt at a big goal:

- Did you succeed?
- Why/why not?
- What worked?

☞ What didn't work?

☞ What did you learn?

☞ What would you do differently if you did it again?

Take some time in a quiet place to ask these questions, and ask anyone else who was part of the action to answer them as well. Sometimes different people can have a completely different experience of the situation. Some people may think you succeeded and others may think you failed for different reasons.

At this point you have the opportunity to get started on the next project! If you have been really going for it, you have probably already seen other exciting opportunities along the way, or even started something new that is still in motion.

If you failed to achieve your goal you could have feelings of resignation, disappointment, apathy, guilt, anger or blame. These are normal feelings, but they are not going to help you create your life or make your dreams come true, so head back to chapter 1 and reacquaint yourself with failure as a step on your path to success. If you are failing, you are one step closer! So get your persistence and determination back, clear your head, make a shiny new goal and start again.

If you succeeded you could be enjoying any number of life-changing experiences right now. Congratulations! I hope this process has shown you that you really do have the ability to change your life completely, to design your life and to make your dreams come true. Things may be different or bigger or smaller than you imagined, but you created a goal and then did what you could to make it a reality. You created a wave of momentum through sheer determination and it altered how you feel about yourself and how you live your life.

Harnessing this understanding and refusing to give up on your dreams and goals when faced with failure will make you one of those successful people others aspire to be like. The more you courageously put yourself out there, the more confidence and experience you will get, and every once in a while something incredible will happen as a result and changes your life forever.

A final word on success

Your life is precious, and you never know how much of it you are going to get. So get yourself out there, make the most of it and die fulfilled, knowing you did everything you could to create something wonderful. In my eyes, that is the true meaning of both life and success.

You now understand how to succeed in creating a life you love. Many of us get stopped by the steps to making our dreams a reality. So while the ideas in this book are not groundbreaking, I hope you can now see clear steps to creating projects that will change your life and make your dreams something you can enjoy each day.

I can't promise you that it will be easy, but it is definitely possible if you are willing to do what it takes.

Here is a summary of the steps we have discussed for creating life-changing projects. Although it seems simple, every successful person in the world follows a similar plan when embarking on an exciting new project.

1   *Create an idea for a project that would absolutely change your life if you were to succeed.* This step is all about creating an idea so exciting that it will keep you going when you are tired, uncertain, stressed or overwhelmed. These things may happen from time to time and are normal emotions to feel when taking on a life-changing project.

2   *Get started.* This is where you stop being a dreamer and start being someone who makes your dreams come true! You have to start somewhere, even if you don't know how it will turn out — even if you have

no experience or lack the resources you think you will need. When starting out make a list of actions that you can take. It could be as simple as calling some people who may be able to help you expand your ideas, or creating a rough plan that you can share with people you think may be interested.

3   *Make a public declaration.* This is where you tell people about your goals. Think about your communities. You could share your idea with your friends on social media, call your family or create a blog to keep people updated. Build a community that has some emotional investment in seeing you succeed.

4   *Get a coach, a mentor or someone who will hold you accountable.* Find someone you can report to on a regular basis — someone who is committed to supporting you through the whole challenge, who can see your potential and who can help you overcome problems and solve challenges as they come up. Find your 'person' as soon as possible and have them agree to work with you regularly. If they do not fulfil your needs, keep looking until you find someone who will.

5   *Take every action you know to take.* This is where you just keep working on your project, every day, in every spare moment you get. With your end goal in mind, look at daily or weekly goals that will take you one step closer. If you feel overwhelmed, you are probably looking too far ahead. Just do what you can do today. Tomorrow you can worry about tomorrow.

6   *Surround yourself with like-minded people.* If you find that this project requires you to think differently, your existing friends and community may not understand what you are going through. Get online and discover the events, courses, forums and networks where you

will find people who are on the same journey as you. This includes joining the Facebook group: www.in12months.com/success-facebook-group.

7   *Approach each challenge with creative solutions.* For every challenge there is a solution. For any big, seemingly impossible challenges, sit down and brainstorm possible solutions, go wild with potential solutions and then work on making them happen. Be creative, cheeky, persistent and outrageous when coming up with solutions. If you can't think of a solution you either need to be more creative or let go of your expectation that it has to be a certain way. There are multiple solutions; you just need to figure them out and then get into action to make them work.

8   *Take every action that you can think of.* This old chestnut! You should by now have realised that taking action will take you somewhere. On the way, you will find more opportunities and more chances of success. If you are not taking action, you have closed the door on the possibilities of your project. If you are stuck, write a list of actions that will help you succeed and then tick them off one at a time as you do them.

9   *Succeed or fail.* Understand what worked and didn't work. Whether you succeed or fail in your current project, or at different stages of your project, it is important that you pause and reflect on what it is that's working and not working that got you to this point. This will help you build on what is working and learn from what didn't work. This process is essential if you are to move on and achieve great things — or more great things! It enables you to clear the slate and turn failures into learning opportunities.

10   *Regroup and start again.* You may have failed and
     learned some valuable lessons. You may have
     succeeded and life is a little bit (or a lot) more
     exciting than it was before. Either way, this is not the
     end of the journey! This is the bit where you get to
     expand again with a new goal, a new idea and a new
     life-changing project. You now have experience that
     you didn't have before you started. This gives you a
     head start and may inspire your next project. This is
     the bit where you get to cement your life as the life of
     someone who follows many or all of their dreams and
     makes them a reality.

Of course, the only way to do this is to get started and take
action towards your next life-changing adventure today!

Index

action takers 34–35 *see also* action, taking

action, taking 5–6, 8, 20, 23, 34–39, 66–69, 71–82, 94, 164 *see also* action takers
— by overcoming procrastination 77–82

Almerico, Kendall 138–140

'anything is possible' habit 55

backup tools 182–184

blog ambassadors program 91, 144, 190

blogging, for publicity 98, 113, 187, 206

blogs, targeting other 75, 139, 174, 175

Bowness, Mark (Life Change— The Revolution) 45–46

bucket lists 36–38, 62

budgeting 132–136

business/career checklist 18–20

challenges, overcoming 54–57, 107–108, 159, 163–180

change 178–189
— embracing 9–39, 50, 57
— life-changing goals 42–44, 61–63
— mindset for 4–6

coaches 75, 81, 100, 121, 153–154, 161, 167, 169, 206 *see also* mentors

comfort zone, stepping out of 100–102, 106, 117–118, 120

commitment, achieving and maintaining 109–116, 164–165, 168–169

completing projects *see* wrapping up projects

communication with team 158–159

community, building a 63, 67, 81, 104, 149, 157, 206
community, nurturing your 13, 53, 73, 75, 99, 187 *see also* public relations
confidence, gaining 117–119
— recipe for 119–121
courage *see* confidence
creating opportunities 97–98
crowdfunding 136–140
Crowdfund Insider 138–140
crucial elements, for projects 66–67
— and key actions 67–68

databases, building 176
Davidof, Susanna (SunChild Collective) 56
debts 17, 32, 33, 130–131, 136
designing your life 1–8
— deciding on the results you want to achieve 59–60
— creating milestones 64–66
— crucial elements 66–68
— setting life-changing goals 61–63
— setting a timeframe 63–64
documentaries, making 46, 61–62, 89, 118–119, 134–136, 190, 192, 197 *see also* videos, creating
dreams 32–33 *see also* goals
— bucket lists 36–38, 62
— freedom to follow 2–5
— overcoming excuses 34–35
— overcoming negative thoughts 26, 49–50

— taking action towards 5–6, 8, 20, 23, 34–39, 66–69, 71–82, 94, 164
— using talents to achieve 38–39
Dropbox 183

education *see* learning
Elance 185
email marketing 140, 142, 146–147, 176
email, professional appearance of 181–182
emotions, overcoming 175–176
employees 126–127 *see also* teams
Endangered Wildlife Trust 194
Entrepreneur.com 138
evaluation of projects 203–205
excuses, overcoming 34–35
expatriation *see* living overseas

Facebook marketing 139, 140, 187, 195, 207
failure *see also* risk, embracing
— embracing 35, 43, 44, 47–49
— seven reasons for 163–169
Ferris, Timothy 1
finances *see* money management
Five Point Five 61, 63, 65, 67, 76, 89–90, 96, 118, 119, 134, 144, 152, 179–180
— 12-month diary 189–202
Fiverr 185

focus, maintaining 78–79, 80, 164–165
The 4-Hour Workweek (book) 1
freedom
— life of 2–4
— as mindset 4–5
freelancers, employing 185–186
funding 132–133
— through competitions 56
— crowd funding 68, 136–140
— fundraising 66, 68, 98, 140–143
— grants 138, 146
— marketing 146–147
— sponsorship/partnership 143–145

goals, to achieve success *see also* dreams
— creating 36–37, 41–42, 61–63
— life-changing 42–46
— milestones, creating 64–66
— timeframe, setting 63–64
Good Life Crisis 7–8, 42
GoToWebinar 187
grants 138, 146

habits, productive 80–81
headspace, creating the right 78–79
health checklist 28–31
Hearne, Andrew (Near River Produce) 52–53

Howlett, Randal (Condor Trekkers) 85–86
How to Retire in 12 Months (book) 100, 130

languages, learning 91, 102, 106, 191, 193, 195
leadership 11, 71, 104, 110, 157–159, 161, 167–177
— and personality types 159–161
learning
— and knowledge as distraction 93–95
— of languages 91, 102, 106, 191, 193, 195
— from mistakes 156
— and need for 88–93
life-changing goals 42–44
— creating 29, 61–63
— mindset 68–69
life coaching *see* coaches
lifestyle checklist 9–32
— business/career checklist 18–20
— finances checklist 15–18
— health checklist 28–31
— personal satisfaction checklist 24–27
— quality of life checklist 21–23
— relationship checklist 11–14
lifestyle design *see* designing your life
limitations, overcoming 62–63, 99
living overseas 85–86 *see also* travelling

ManageWP 183
marketing your project 76, 96,
135, 144, 145, 146–147,
153, 171, 172, 174–176
— email 140, 142, 146–147,
176
— Facebook 139, 140, 187,
195, 207
marketing your project (cont'd)
— publications 75, 144, 175,
191
— publicity 74–76, 139–140
— public relations 144,
175–176, 190, 206
— radio 75, 76, 145, 153,
172, 174, 197
— social media 75, 76, 96,
139, 140, 146–147, 201
— television 75
— Twitter 98, 139, 184, 187
meditation 50, 79, 128
mentors 57, 75, 98, 153–155,
162, 169 see also coaches
milestones, setting 64–66,
190
the million dollar measure
127–128
MiNDFOOD (magazine) 144,
191
mindset, change 4–5, 7, 26,
42, 43–44, 57, 73–74, 107
momentum, building 74–76,
84–85, 86–88, 94, 95
money management 45–46,
52–53, 73–74, 129–147
— budgeting 132–136
— debts 17, 32, 33,
130–131, 136
— funding 136–147

Moolenschot, Catherine
(Inspire Greatness) 155

need-to-know list 88–93
networks, professional 75, 76,
136, 156–157, 206–207 see
also relationships
Neuro-Linguistic Programming
(NLP) 100

opportunities, creating 97–98
organised, being 181–187

partnerships 143–144, 145, 157
PayPal 186
Pedersen, Tracey (Life
Changing Year) 178
personal relationships 11, 21,
75, 110, 114, 128, 139, 142,
154, 156–157, 169
personal satisfaction checklist
24–27
prioritising 103–104
procrastination,
overcoming 77–78
— and headspace 78–79
— productive habits 80–81
— support system 81–82
— through technology 79–80
publications, marketing
through 75, 144, 175, 191
professional, looking 181–182
publicity 75–76, 139–140,
175–176 see also public
relations public declaration
of goals 190, 206
public relations 175–176,
190, 206 see also publicity;
community, nurturing your

public speaking, overcoming fear of 100–102

quality of life 21–23

radio marketing 75, 76, 145, 153, 172, 174, 197
recruitment 104–105, 152–153, 158–162
rejection, dealing with 97–98
relationships *see also* support system; networks, professional
— community 8, 11, 13, 53, 67, 73–74, 81, 104, 119, 157, 175, 206
— mentors 57, 75, 98, 153–155, 162, 169
— personal 11, 21, 75, 110, 114, 128, 139, 142, 154, 156–157, 169
— relationship checklist 11–14
resources 181–187
risk, embracing 35, 43–44, 47–49, 117–118 *see also* failure
roadblocks to projects 176–178
Robinson, Pania (Joyful Soil) 73–74
Roboform 183
Rode Microphones 144, 190

Safar, Lee 6
sales, managing 186
Skyrocket Marketing 144
social media marketing
— Facebook 139, 140, 187, 195, 207
— Twitter 98, 139, 184, 187

SourceBottle 175–176
sponsorship 143–145
success
— defining 46–47
— practical steps towards 103–108
— what you need to achieve 7–8
support system *see also* relationships 149–162

taking action *see* action, taking
talents, using to achieve goals 38–39
teams *see also* employees
— leading 158–162
— recruiting of 104–105, 152–153, 158–162
television 75
timeframe, setting 63–64
time management 123–126
— for employees 126–127
— and the million dollar measure 127–128
— for parents 126
tragedy, as catalyst for change 43–44
travelling 1, 33, 64, 96, 189–202 *see also* living overseas
— long term 1, 91, 108, 177–178
— and working 1, 56, 61, 63
Tribe Wanted 45–46
troubleshooting 163–180
12-month diary 189–202
Twitter marketing 98, 139, 184, 187

unroll 185

videos, creating 65, 67, 76,
    89–91, 134, 138–139,
    171, 191–192 *see also*
    documentaries, making
virtual assistants, employing 185
visualisation, of goal 115–116

webinars 187
Website Launchpad 182
websites, tools for creating
    182, 183

working and travelling 1, 56,
    61, 63
the world clock meeting
    planner 184
World Vision 90–91, 144, 190,
    199–200
WP SuperGeek 153
wrapping up projects
    203–205

YouTube 187

ZohoMail 182

You finished the book!

So... What's Next?!

For more help and support, consider...

Coaching
Work with Serena one-on-one! Get clarity and confidence for your projects and ideas.

Courses
Join one of Serena's live web-based courses and learn step-by-step how to kick start your blog, website or book.

How to Retire in 12 Months—Book
In this bestseller you will discover why and how you can create a new lifestyle by building a community online.

Subscribe
to *www.in12months.com* and *www.fivepointfive.org* for free eBooks, resources and regular new content.

Connect with Serena
Email *serena@in12months.com* with questions and get your project moving!

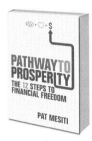